# Launching
# Your
# Preschooler

### Ways to Help Your Child in His First Experiences

# By Edgar S. Bley

### Illustrated by Doug Anderson

**STERLING PUBLISHING CO., Inc.**

New York

© Copyright, 1955, by
Sterling Publishing Company, Inc.
419 Fourth Avenue, New York 16, N. Y.

*All Rights Reserved*

Manufactured in the United States of America
Type set by Atlantic Linotype Co., Brooklyn, N. Y.

Library of Congress Catalog Card No. 55-10381

SBN: 8069–0072–5

# CONTENTS

# 1. "The First Time"

When I was a small child, my grandfather grew impatient with my efforts at learning to swim. "You ought to take him out to deep water and throw him in," the old gentleman advocated. "Then he'll learn how to swim. That's what they did to me when I was a boy!"

Fortunately for me, no one took his advice seriously. How successful this method was for him might be judged (though he never mentioned it) by the fact that no man living had ever seen Grandpa venture into deep water. His first experience had been too much for him.

The first time is the important time. Put a child on roller skates against his will, or in a situation where he feels disgraced if he cannot skate off like an expert *at once*—and he may never learn to roller skate in his life. Watch a child whose "first time" on skates has been handled more happily, learning to roller skate, ignoring bruised elbows and skinned knees, wobbling, falling, getting up and wobbling some more. He'll learn! The old proverb, "If at first you don't succeed, try, try again," suits this situation to a tee—but it would not have applied had the child been unwilling or too young—or in the swimming situation my grandfather starred in.

In many, many situations it is the first experience which counts. If a child's first visit to a dentist consists of a jolly conversation, an examination that is neither painful nor frightening, and a brand new toothbrush to top it off, his ensuing visits will be easy for him. If his first independent shopping trip—to the familiar corner store for a loaf of bread—comes off without mishap, he will be eager to go shopping another time. There is another proverb, perhaps of more recent origin, which says, "Nothing succeeds like success." This one has more psychological truth than the other. Every successful experience increases the likelihood of a repeat performance being successful, too. Further, the more successful experiences a child has in a number of areas, the more likely he is to be successful on moving into a brand new area, since each success helps build self-confidence and independence.

## THE WAY TO INDEPENDENCE

A little child who is never picked up and cuddled when he is hurt may well feel alone in a hostile world. A child who is always snatched up, petted and crooned over, at the least little injury, may feel himself to be helpless and inadequate. The way to independence, obviously, lies at some finely balanced point between these two extremes. Trying to find this balance is a problem which must be solved uniquely by each family.

However, there are innumerable situations that *do not depend on intangible factors,* in which you can help your preschooler achieve independence by means of comparatively simple techniques. It is these situations which are brought out in this book. The simple but effective techniques which are here discussed and illustrated will help increase your security as a parent and thus serve doubly to aid both you and your child.

The situations in themselves involve independence—situations in which your little child has to deal with persons other than his own family, places other than his own home. Stress is placed on the first times he goes to these various places, first times he has to relate to unfamiliar people. It is the first experiences, more than any other, that count in building independence.

## A SIDELIGHT ON "FIRST"

Many of the situations to be discussed as first experiences will be things which your child did during infancy, yet they have become "new" situations again during early childhood. At the age of six months he may have been left at Grandma's in his basket while you went off about your business; yet at two he may object violently to being left there. It suddenly seems new, strange, frightening. In a way he feels, though he could not put it into words, that perhaps you will never return. He has been left with Grandma for the first time *when he can realize what is happening and consider whether or not he approves.* From the point of view of his awareness, this is a first time. To sum up, experience has little value in developing independence until the child has reached an age of awareness, an age at which the experience doesn't simply happen to him but involves *his* thinking and feeling.

It is most important for parents to realize this. Those who do not are constantly being disappointed in what looks like "backsliding" on the part of their little ones. You can hear them anywhere:

"I don't know what's wrong with Jimmy! He's been travelling in trains since he was born, but today he screamed when the train came into the station and he couldn't sit still for a minute during the entire trip!"

"I don't know what's happened to Suzie. She has always loved going to Dr. James, but today she was awful! She cried and screamed and kicked. I was so embarrassed."

"I don't know what's wrong with Betty. She has always been so cute and so good when we had company. But last night she kept clinging to my skirts, and when I had to push her away she ran and hid under her bed!"

"I don't know what's occurred with George. He has always tasted new foods and generally liked them. But today when he had artichokes for the first time, I could hardly get him to take a bite. And when he did, he seemed to have decided in advance that he wouldn't like it!"

Some "first times" are obviously "firsts." You take your preschooler to a building with an elevator and you know perfectly well that he has never ridden on an elevator before. This is easy to recognize, and you naturally take some pains to prepare him for the elevator so that it will be fun, not frightening. But it is harder to recognize that the child who has been riding in an elevator every few months all his life will one day approach it with new awareness—and that this, too, will be a "first time."

# THREE GOLDEN RULES

A successful first experience depends on the child's being *ready* for it.

A successful first experience depends on the child's being *prepared* for it.

A successful first experience depends on the child's being helped to *talk about it afterwards*.

Since these three principles apply to every situation in the book, and to countless other "firsts" not covered in the book, it will be worth while to speak of each of them here. These are principles that nearly all educators and nearly all psychologists will agree on, regardless of their other differences. Likewise, they are principles that parents can and should ask themselves to follow, principles which do not depend on subtle factors in your own personality but which you can follow by simply deciding to do so.

# READINESS

A child is ready for a new experience when he is quite secure in his feelings about less complicated but similar situations. For example, if your four-year-old can go to bed occasionally without his story, or his usual sleeping toy, or a special blanket, or the door and light arranged in just a certain way—then he may be ready to sleep away from home some night. But if he still needs all these props to make him feel safe about a night at home, it would be foolish to attempt a night out.

An important sidelight on readiness is that it must not be confused with desire. Four-year-old Bobby who has been visiting his cousin Suzie doesn't want to go home when you call for him at five o'clock. "Let me sleep here over night," he begs. The more he thinks about it, the more he wants to do it. But this wanting is not sufficient proof of his being ready. If you give in, knowing he is not really ready, you may well have to come and pick him up at eight o'clock—and perhaps postpone by years the time when he will achieve independence in this area.

The difference between the wish and the readiness often causes misunderstanding between parents and primary teachers.

Teacher may know that Johnnie isn't ready to read; the coordination of his eyes has not matured to the point of differentiating between letters. Mama says he is ready to read, because he complains all the time that he *wants* to read. Yet this same mother is not fooled by the fact that Johnnie also *wants* to drive the family car!

## PREPARATION

Preparation for a new experience involves several stages. First, let your child know well in advance what is going to happen. Second, tell him what it will be like, with as many details as seem reasonable. Give him some advance knowledge of how he will be expected to act and how others will probably act toward him. ("Then you will open your mouth very wide and sit very still. The dentist will take a silver stick with a tiny mirror on the end and hold it in your mouth. That's how he can see the backs and sides of your teeth and make sure that everything is all right.")

An important part of preparation is telling your child how he will probably feel—and telling him the truth. The experienced pediatrician doesn't say to a child, "This shot will not hurt." He says, "This will hurt, but only for a minute."

## RECAPITULATION

Recapitulation means talking over what has happened when it is all over. Bobby has spent a week at Grandma's. Talking over those parts of his stay which might have been emotionally difficult helps him see that they worked out all right, makes it easier for him another time:

*Mother*: What did you do when I first left?

*Bobby*: I cried.

*Mother*: And after a while you stopped crying?

*Bobby*: Yes. Grandma gave me a cookie. Then she took me to the store with her and we bought food for supper.

*Mother*: You felt sad for a little while when I first went away, but then you felt fine. What did you have for supper?

Any new experience is likely to have some unpleasant emotional content, ranging anywhere from mere shyness to extreme fear. Talking about them, quite casually, helps him to see that these emotions were normal, reasonable, and more than balanced by the pleasant aspects of the experience. A child with a healthy sense of independence is not necessarily a fearless child, but one who can take a little fear in his stride in order to step out into the world on his own.

# 2. Bobby Goes Visiting

When your preschooler goes visiting with you, he is faced with a number of new problems. There will be a new house, new grounds. There may be new people. New demands will be made upon him:

Aunt Lucy will be delighted to see him, but horrified if he touches any of the bric-a-brac with which her house is festooned.

Aunt Martha doesn't mind what Bobby plays with, and her possessions don't run to the breakable—but she will expect him to say "How do you do?" and ask permission and voice his thanks. She expects him to act like a miniature adult.

Aunt Rebecca doesn't care about fancy manners, but she's a kissing bug. She loves Bobby and feels hurt when he doesn't care to spend the afternoon snuggled in her lap.

Mrs. Jackman believes children should be seen but not heard. She frowns at you whenever Bobby acts his age, and you are torn between your affection for her and the impossibility of changing Bobby into a mid-Victorian model.

Mrs. Winston wants to talk with you about so many exciting things that she can't spare a minute for Bobby. You find it difficult to listen to her and watch your son too.

The Kelmans have a shop full of intriguing—and dangerous—power tools.

The Cullmans have a garden full of appealing flowers that are not to be picked.

The Colemans feel that boys are to be waited on but that girls share in all the household work.

The Callmans feel that girls may act naturally but that boys are little gentlemen who should open doors and hold chairs for the ladies.

Even you, a mature adult, find it a little difficult to go from Aunt Rebecca's house to Aunt Martha's in the same afternoon, from an atmosphere of warmth and casual behavior to one of formality and polite exchange. But you can do it. You know how to find a middle ground between acting the way your hostess expects and "being yourself." For your preschooler, the situation can be confusing, at best—and terrifying at the worst.

## MAKE VISITS BRIEF

Bobby's first visit to any particular household should be very short. Plan everything from a ten-minute call to perhaps a half hour, depending on the degree to which the expectations of that household differ from your own. If your hostess might think this is odd, explain to her in advance—and not in front of Bobby! You needn't feel shy about making life livable for your child.

Simply say, "Bobby hasn't had much experience at visiting, and I'd like to make this call a short one. I want him to get away *before* he gets restless. So don't count on our staying for more than five or ten minutes!"

If this is a new idea to your hostess, no harm done. On the contrary, your own expression of interest in making the visit easy and pleasant for your little one may elicit similar behavior from her.

## WHAT SHALL I TAKE THERE?

Plan in advance, with your child, what he will do to pass the time during the visit. In most cases, it is well to take something along.

"Let's take this new book from the library and your Teddy Bear. Mrs. Wilson has a little armchair that will make a perfect bed for Teddy Bear, and we can ask her for a tea towel for a blanket. And then, after you have tucked Teddy in, you can read him the picture book."

Plan some play activity which is really intriguing. Just taking the toy along is not enough. Otherwise your child will most likely drop Teddy Bear in a corner, in favor of investigating your host's prize African violets.

Whenever possible, plan alternatives:

"When you get tired of being very quiet in the living room, you can play in Aunt Sarah's cellar."

"If you get tired of playing on the lawn, you can take a walk around the block."

"If you get hungry on the train home, I'll have a secret supply of cookies in my pocketbook for you."

The more limited the surroundings, the more you will need to supply. One toy might be more than ample if you are visiting in a big house with gardens and fields around it; a shopping bag filled with a great variety of playthings is good insurance when you call on Mrs. Smith in her two-room apartment, or wherever you go on a rainy day.

Don't be surprised if your child's attention span is much shorter while on a visit than at home. The toy which is ordinarily good for an hour may hold him for only three minutes at Grandma's house. This is quite natural. A child has a long attention span only in familiar, perfectly safe surroundings. Grownups react in much the same way. Remember those times when you have picked up a book waiting your turn at the doctor's—how disjointedly you read, compared with the times when you stretch out with a book on your own bed!

## WHAT WILL THE VISIT BE LIKE?

In telling your preschooler what his hostess is like, and in giving him an idea how she will behave, you will also be helping him to know how he should behave.

"When we get to the Reynolds', I'll introduce you to Mrs. Reynolds. She'll say, 'Well, how do you do, Bobby?' And you'll say, 'How do you do, Mrs. Reynolds.' Let's practice. I'll be Mrs. Reynolds and you be Bobby. How do you do, Bobby?"

Or this:

"As soon as we get to Aunt Rebecca's, you give her a great big kiss and a great big hug, and then say, 'May I play in the attic, please, Aunt Becky?' And do you know what she'll say? I'll bet she'll say, 'Bless your heart, of course you may!' "

Or:

"Uncle Dudley will probably want to shake hands with you, won't he? Do you remember the trick about shaking hands? That's right, keep your four fingers together but stick your thumb straight up. Let's try it now. Thumb up!"

Or:

"When we get to Miss Woodward's house, she'll probably give you a glass of milk and a cookie, and you will have to say, 'Thank you.' It's very important, so please remember. Some people don't mind if you forget to say thanks, but not Miss Woodward. She'll mind very much."

## FINDING THINGS ON A MOMENT'S NOTICE

Sometimes you will drop in for a visit, together with your youngster, without having planned it in advance. Or perhaps a projected ten-minute visit is unavoidably prolonged. Then you will need to find something for the child to do, even if it involves some slight inconvenience to your host. Prepare for this *before* the young one becomes bored and restless.

If your child is two or three years old, a kitchen sink half filled with soapy water and some measuring cups, egg beaters and other utensils should be good for half an hour's fun. Line the floor with newspaper, in advance.

Or, if that seems too messy and more noise is not especially objectionable, many two-year-olds would be happy with an assortment of pots and pans with a wooden spoon for a drumstick.

Most threes and all fours and fives can string odd beads or the contents of your hostess' button box. Just provide a not-too-sharp needle threaded with a long piece of the coarsest thread available.

Three- and four-year-old children in an emergency can be given an old magazine and a pair of scissors. If your youngster is five or six, the same materials will do, but some directions can make the activity more interesting: "Why don't you cut out all

the pictures of automobiles you can find?" Or flowers, or whatever will appeal to your child, Choose something that appears sufficiently often in the available magazines.

In situations like this (as in many another) it is a good idea to say directly and positively to your child, "Here is an old magazine and a pair of scissors. Sit down now at this table and cut pictures." This is much better than to ask, "Would you like to cut pictures?" and risk getting a negative response. Naturally, if Bobby really doesn't want to do it, it would be foolish to insist, but it is much easier for him to agree to a very firmly stated suggestion than to an open question.

## THE AFTER-TALK

Managing an unfamiliar situation and dealing with new people and places, give your child a feeling of independence. They broaden his horizons. He sees that the world is bigger than his own home—and that he can cope with it. For these reasons, it is not only important that you help him in every way to have a successful experience, but also that you help him *feel* successful about it.

After the visit, talk it over. With a two- or three- or even four-year-old, you can go over almost everything that happened. Enumerate especially those aspects of the visit that most differ from life at home. For example:

"That was a big house, wasn't it? It was much bigger than our house. Did you ever see a house with so many rooms? There were lots of places for you to run and explore. You can't do that in our little house, can you?"

"You were very clever to sit so still for so long at Mrs. Johnson's house. It wasn't much fun, was it? But that's what you have to do sometimes, when you go out visiting. Wasn't that strawberry ice cream good?"

"At Aunt Rhoda's house everybody kisses everybody when they come and when they go. Did you ever have so many kisses in one day?"

"It's hard to remember that you can't touch so many things, when you're visiting other people. But you did very well. And you didn't fuss when I reminded you."

If some things went wrong, don't harp on them. If they are worth mentioning at all, it is probably more effective in the long run to comfort your child about his misdemeanors than to increase his feelings of failure or guilt:

"I wouldn't worry too much about knocking over that glass of milk. Everyone knocks things over, at times. I know I seemed angry at the time, but that was foolish. After all, I knock things over sometimes, too, don't I?"

Occasionally, of course, you will end a visit with the feeling that you don't want to take Bobby calling again for at least five years. Everything went wrong and he was a continual nuisance. To try and hide your feelings is not a good idea, since Bobby will undoubtedly be aware of them and will feel more guilty if they are not brought out in the open. However, it is often possible (if you count to ten and take a deep breath before you speak) to do it with good grace and with some humor:

"Well, that was pretty hard going, wasn't it? But we got out of it alive, anyway. I can't say much more for it."

Or:

"We certainly destroyed the peace and quiet of the Jackson home, didn't we? Do you know what they're probably doing now? Lying back in their chairs and sighing with relief that our visit is over."

Or try to see where *you* went wrong in your planning:

"That wasn't much fun for you, was it? Next time I'll take along more toys so that you'll really have something to do. Then you won't have to complain and fuss so much when the grownups are talking. What toy would you like to take along the next time we go visiting?"

## REPEAT VISITS

The suggestions given above do not apply only to first visits. To some extent, they should serve for all visiting with your pre-schooler and even with your six- or seven-year-old. The more often you visit a particular family, the better you will know what to do to insure the visit's being a success for your child. After a few times, his behavior will fall into a particular pattern for each home you visit.

Thus you will soon realize that at the Bernstein's he will play in the back yard, at Aunt Stella's he will sit on a certain hassock and look at books his cousin had as a child, at the O'Neil's he will play in the attic, and at Aunt Ruth's he won't find anything to do at all unless you take something with you.

If you discover that visits at certain households are rarely or never successful, there are two courses to follow. Don't take Bobby to that house until he is much older. Or arrange to visit there when he is home in bed, visiting friends of his own, or other-wise occupied. However, a difficult situation may come about with near relatives or very close friends whom you wish to visit often and who would be hurt if you came without the little one. There is an almost foolproof way of handling this kind of situation:

Get one or several very intriguing playthings, different from those which your youngster has at home. Choose toys that can be used in many different ways. Arrange for these to be left at the home to be visited for your child's use while visiting. Remind him, before a visit, that now he will have a chance to play with the Tinker-toy, or the sleepy doll, or the dump truck, or whatever it may be. After the visit, refer to these toys again. Be sure not to let him take any toy home with him, even if he protests that he is "in the middle of the game," or that he prefers this toy to any he has at home. The fact that he cannot take it along, cannot play with it often enough or long enough to grow bored with it, is the secret of its success.

There is another advantage to the "toy at Grandma's" idea. Young children find it very difficult to share their possessions, and it is open to question whether it is desirable to try to make them. But if Grandma keeps several toys at her house which are played with by all her visiting grandchildren, then your little one has a chance to do some preliminary sharing *in absentia*. He is not there while Cousin Margaret is using the doll or Cousin Jack building with the blocks, but he can be told that these toys are for him and all his cousins, whoever happens to be visiting: "Grandma says that Jack has as much fun building with these blocks as you do, whenever he comes to visit!"

## DINING OUT

Just as first visits (and to some degree nearly all visits) are difficult for your preschooler, visits which include a meal are doubly hard. There are several reasons for this. One has to do with the child's own emotional life. Eating is a very vital and intimate part of a child's existence. His first affection tie with his mother is related to being fed by her. Until he is well in his teens, being fed continues to occupy the central position in his family membership.

For this reason, the young child surrounds his eating with ritual. He objects highly to having his place at the table changed. He insists on a certain spoon, a certain bowl, a certain glass. He is doubtful about tasting new foods and often reacts quite violently. Not only is the child emotional about his eating, but his eating arouses strong emotion in his parents, too. This explains why so many parents, reasonable in other aspects of child-rearing, set up such strong positions in regard to food: Bobby must eat every bite on his plate. Or, Bobby must never be asked to eat anything he doesn't want. It explains, too, why "feeding problems" are so prevalent, at both ends of the scale. For months, or perhaps years, Bobby hardly eats enough to keep a bird alive. Or, Bobby is too fat already but he just can't stop eating.

The other thing that makes eating out hard on your preschooler is that your hosts usually have their own definite ideas about table manners, proper eating procedures, and so forth.

Eating in a household where meals are no more formal than at home won't be too much of a problem. But in many childless families, or families in which the children are already grown up, the table is likely to be much more formal than the situation in which your youngster ordinarily eats.

One problem is the duration of a meal, when you are a guest. If your little one is called to the table too long before he can actually begin to eat, he will be restless sooner than necessary. Explain to your hostess that it will be better to call Bobby in just as she starts to serve, or just before grace if one is to be said. Better yet, ask her (in advance) to serve Bobby first and allow him to start right in. When he has finished his main course, why not excuse him from the table—and from the room—until dessert is served? Even if at home he is used to remaining at the table throughout the meal, this one will undoubtedly be slower, with more adult conversation.

It is often better to let him eat separately, before the others. If you don't want to trouble your hostess with this arrangement, ask her to let *you* set up his meal and sit with him while he eats it. (You might even bring along his food.) Many times a youngster having been fed in advance, under easy circumstances, will then feel quite "safe" about eating in this house and will come to the dinner table and eat all over again with the grownups. Otherwise, it's a good idea to have some food that he can eat, during the adult meal, like dry cereal or a box of animal crackers.

Just as you may have to protect your child from the hostess' adult expectations about remaining long at the table, you will need to protect him from her adult expectations about the amount he will eat. Most children, most of the time, eat very little when dining out. Unless you are sure that your hostess will serve a suitably small portion, ask permission to serve Bobby yourself. If the hostess feels he is not eating enough, explain to her that it is perfectly all right, that children often skip a meal or two and make it up at another time. If your child is embarrassed by repeated invitations to have some more, answer for him. "No, thanks. Bobby doesn't want any more roast beef. He has had plenty." Sometimes you will need to help get a platter passed his way. "Would you like a piece of bread, Bobby? All right. Mrs. Wylie, will you please pass the bread to Bob?"

## GETTING READY TO EAT OUT

As with other visits, dining out requires advance preparation. Tell as many details as you can: in which room you will eat, next to whom Bobby will sit, how the food will be served. Tell him what will be expected in the way of manners. If possible, tell him what there will be to eat. If he needn't remain at the table throughout the meal, plan with him what he will do while the grownups are eating. But be sure to help him realize that dining out is considered a pleasure, that the food will be good and that you expect to enjoy it.

If something special in the way of table manners will be demanded, it's a good idea to practice them once at home. "Let's make believe that our lunch is really dinner at Uncle Bob's. I'll be Uncle Bob, because he always serves. Ready? (Imitating a masculine voice:) How about scrambled eggs, Bobby? Big, small, or enormous?"

In some households, what Bobby eats is unimportant, as long

as he is quiet and polite at the table. In others, manners count for little, but what matters is that he eat like a horse. Help him know what is important to his hostess. He, like you, will be anxious to please if only he knows clearly what will be pleasing.

## VISITING WITHOUT YOU

The ability to enjoy visiting is a mark of independence of spirit, for your preschooler, but when he can visit without you he will have accomplished a degree of actual, physical independence. This step will be achieved best after he has learned to handle simple visiting with ease, self-assurance and pleasure. Even then, it will need careful introduction, just as in the case of first visits along with you.

(1) Choose that household in which he is most relaxed and best occupied. Boredom is the first ingredient of loneliness, and that is what you must avoid. On the day you are to leave him there, take extra care in providing him with something that is fun to do.

(2) Tell him before you embark on the visit that while you are visiting the Smiths, you are going to leave him there for five or ten minutes while you go to the store. (Perhaps you can make your departure rather desirable by going for a quart of ice cream or something else that he will share in, on your return.) Be specific about what store you are going to and what you intend to buy there. Show it to him, after you return, so that he is sure you were telling the literal truth.

(3) Tell him again, before you leave. Say you will be gone five minutes, or ten. If necessary, and if he can read the clock even partially, show him the minute hand and show him where it will be when you return. Explain that if he needs anything during your absence, Mrs. Smith will be glad to help him.

(4) Make sure that your errand takes no longer than you have said it would.

(5) Talk about it, both after your return from the errand and again when the entire visit is over.

## BUILDING UP HIS CAPACITY

This kind of brief departure taking place in the middle of a longer visit is an excellent beginning. If it works well, try it several times. When your child feels really confident about this situation, try him for an hour or so. In each case, make it clear that you are visiting Mrs. Smith, too, not simply "dropping him at the Smiths" while you go about your own business.

However, that too should be possible, as his independence increases. If you have gradually built toward it, taking each step only after he has come to feel entirely safe about the previous step, the day will come when you can say, "I have to go to Dr. Williams' office this morning, and I'm going to take you to visit Aunt Emily while I'm gone." This, obviously, is the final step. If he can do it successfully, he is behaving like an adult in this area of experience, since now he is not merely being independent during a portion of a family visit, but he himself is the sole visitor.

## THE IMPORTANCE OF ALL THIS

It might seem that this is a great deal of work in order to gain a small accomplishment. You may well think, "Why go through all this preparation, just so that Bobby can visit someone without me. If it takes so much doing, he needn't go visiting until he is older, and he can learn independence in other areas."

All this is true, except for one vital consideration. The day may come when you have to leave Bobby at someone's house, for reasons beyond your control. If this should come about, it will probably happen without advance notice, and there will then be no time to do a careful build-up. You will simply have to drop him at Grandma's and go hurrying off to the hospital, or some other emergency, hoping against hope that he can take it.

Bobby's independence is not only a sign of maturity in him—it is also a kind of insurance for you, against that possible emergency.

A mother was planning to leave her little daughter with an aunt while she went to the hospital to have a new baby. She had planned to use the last month of her pregnancy to accustom the little girl to staying with the aunt. However, the new baby was premature by a month and no preparation was possible. How much better if independence in this area had been developed earlier, before it was acutely needed.

On a much older level, many a teacher gets her class accustomed to functioning in her absence, partly to develop a kind of group independence, partly so that the children will be able to handle themselves well on the occasions when she will have to absent herself from the classroom. Often she will leave the room while they are busy with a task that doesn't require her constant presence, stroll down the hall, and be back before they have had time to get into trouble. After a while they accept the fact that they are able to work while she is away—and they feel good about themselves, as a result. What this teacher is doing with her eight-, ten- or twelve-year-olds is the same thing you are doing with your preschooler.

## OVERNIGHT VISITING

Many little children express the desire to stay overnight with a cousin or a friend, long before they are really ready to do so. Most often the desire is avid in the late afternoon, much paler by the time supper is over, and vanished completely before bedtime. Few preschoolers are comfortable about sleeping away from their parents; in more cases, readiness for this step arrives somewhere between the ages of eight and twelve.

However, there are circumstances which might make it desirable to help your little one reach this stage sooner. For one thing, there is the ever-present possibility that an emergency might make it necessary for him to stay away overnight—or over several nights. For some children who do not go to nursery school and who happen to have no friends of suitable age and temperament in the neighborhood, sleeping at a friend's may be the best way for him to have more than sporadic companionship.

An easy way to begin, if the other child happens to be more ready than your child, is to have the friend sleep at your house once or twice. Talk to your youngster, later, about how his friend felt. Was it funny for him to sleep in a strange bed? To be tucked in by you instead of his own mother? But wasn't it fun for him, all in all?

After several such visits, you might have the friend (rather than you) be the one to suggest a return visit. Simply say, "We love to have you stay here overnight. Would you like Bobby to stay overnight at your house some time?" And when he says yes, say, "Well, you tell him that you want him to come." Grownups resent having words put in their mouths, but children rarely do. Chances are that at the first opportunity he'll tell Bobby to come visit him for a sleep-over.

Even this is not foolproof—and perhaps there will not be a friend ready to take the first step. How can you go about helping your child sleep away from home?

## STEPS TOWARD A SLEEP-OVER

Probably the best all-round way to start the sleep-over habit, if the circumstances permit it, is for you to sleep overnight along with him, once or twice. In this way he will have a chance to get used to the strange place before he has to do it alone.

Country houses, with plenty of room, make this method simple. Two families, one with a four-year-old boy and one with a six-, lived several miles apart. The boys got along well together, and neither had any other children living closer. The times the families could get the boys together were comparatively few, and they knew the frequency could be increased if the boys could take turns sleeping over.

After several verbal attempts to interest one boy or the other in such a scheme, they decided to take the bull by the horns. One day the four-year-old, his mother and his baby sister came visiting at the other house and all slept over. A few days later, the six-year-old and his parents returned the overnight visit. From that day on both boys found it easy and fun to sleep over at each other's house.

Where your child cannot be accompanied by you, or by an

older brother or sister, for his first sleep-over, there is another technique worth trying. Several times when you visit Aunt Margaret, go in the evening and explain to your child in advance that he will take his pajamas, go to bed there while you have an evening visit, and that when it is time to go home you will pick him up and take him home. If you drive your own car, it is not even necessary to dress him when it is time to go home; simply wrap him up, as he is, and carry him to the car. Some children can be gotten up, driven home, and placed in their own beds without being awakened—but this is not necessary, of course.

Talk about this plan in advance, both before leaving home and upon arrival at his aunt's house. Show him the bed in which he'll sleep. Read him his story at bedtime, just as you would at home. Hand him the stuffed animal or whatever he generally sleeps with. Try to make the entire bed-putting as homelike as possible. Don't be upset if he comes out of the bedroom several times, with different excuses. Quite rightly, he wants to check and see that you are really there. If necessary, stay with him until he falls asleep.

After several such episodes, you might tell him one day that you are going to Aunt Margaret's for the evening and that he will go to sleep there, as usual, but that this time you won't bother to get him up and disturb his sleep. This time he can just go on sleeping, and he'll wake up at Aunt Margaret's house and have pancakes for breakfast, and after breakfast you'll come for him. Since it is not urgent to have this go through, don't push the plan if his initial response is negative. One unsuccessful try may delay for years his eventual achievement of sleeping out. However, if circumstances require his staying at Aunt Margaret's, make this clear to him. It is much easier for a child to accomplish something difficult when he knows there is no choice than if he thinks there is.

One word of warning: Do not put your child to bed in someone else's house under the impression that you are going to take him home with you later, and leave him there overnight instead. It may gain a quick victory. He'll sleep there overnight. But his loss of confidence in your word will cause problems for him and for you far outweighing that easy triumph.

# TOILETING AWAY FROM HOME

A problem for some preschoolers, related to eating and sleeping away from home, involves going to the toilet in strange places. This can be very inconvenient from day to day. More serious, it can remain with a person all his life, so that as an adult, although he obviously can manage the situation, he never feels quite comfortable about it.

A survey of thousands of junior high school pupils in a large city, several years ago, indicated that about ten per cent of the boys and over thirty per cent of the girls made a practice of not using school toilets, going unrelieved from before nine in the morning until reaching home after three o'clock. This situation is obviously unhealthy psychologically, and perhaps harmful to physical health as well.

Actually, there is little you can do to help your preschooler overcome this diffidence. It probably depends largely on your having had a relaxed attitude toward toileting while he was an infant. One comforting thing you can do is to go with your little child to the bathroom, away from home, and stay with him until he is finished. Also, it is a good idea *not* to give him the impression that toilets away from home are likely to be unclean.

In general, it is good for you to be aware of the possibility of a problem in this area so you can be alert and helpful. Since you now know that the problem is common, you need not feel chagrinned about being faced with it.

# 3. Helping Betty When Visitors Come

Though most new situations occur away from home, there are "new" events that take place in your own house which demand independence on your child's part. Certain relatives and close friends may have been coming to your house since Betty was too little to remember, so dealing with these people should never be a problem. But there may be some special cases: formal visits, baby sitters, long-time or permanent guests (as when an older relative comes to live with you), and the most permanent "guest" of all—a new baby.

Except with your most constant and casual guests, visitors cause Betty a certain amount of strain similar to that which she experiences on visits. She still has to cope with the varying personalities and expectations of various people. If Mrs. Jackman, as a hostess, expects children to be seen but not heard, she will have similar expectations as your guest. Aunt Martha will expect elegant manners and Aunt Rebecca will want innumerable kisses at your house, just as they do at home.

This means that, with almost every guest, you will need to prepare your child in advance with some notion of the kind of person visiting and how she will be expected to behave. Of course, in your own home you need go less far in the direction of a compromise than you probably do when calling. It is easy to say, at home, "We reserve 'Please' for special occasions and don't insist on it with every little request." Or, "A child this young has to request so many things that an older child would manage for himself, the 'Pleases' would really clutter up her speech." Or you can say, "We don't do so much kissing in our house. You were lucky to get one kiss on your arrival, and if your luck holds out, she may give you another when you leave."

Also, for almost any visit, you will do well to plan in advance how Betty will spend her time—and where. Entertaining Aunt Margaret may be a sufficient occupation for you, but not for Betty. Help her avoid the twin difficulties that little children face when Mother has a guest—the problem of how to spend some time with the grownups, and the problem of how to get away from them.

The most reasonable technique is to let her share the beginning of the visit. After five or ten minutes, but before she begins to be restless, take her to her room, the kitchen, the yard, or somewhere where you have set up a really intriguing occupation for her —painting or finger painting, digging with a new spade in the sand box. Tell her you will call her when there is something to eat. Let her help serve the refreshments. After she has shared in the food, get her going on something interesting again, whether the same thing she was doing before you served or a new one. She might be called in again in time to say goodbye to the guest, or better yet, take the guest to where she is playing for this purpose.

Incidentally, when looking for that engrossing occupation to keep your little one from spending her afternoon hanging on the edges of an adult conversation, don't overlook the long "playing bath." A preschooler who has baths only for cleanliness is unfortunate. The bath for fun is more rewarding. Liven it with a few drops of vegetable coloring, from time to time, or make a bubble bath (perhaps by means of a tablespoonful of detergent), and use all kinds of kitchen utensils and anything that floats for an endless variety of toys.

## WITH FORMAL GUESTS

More trying for your preschooler will be those times when you receive formal calls. If the call is formal but brief, such as a visit by the minister or a new neighbor, it may not be necessary to involve your child at all. Have your visit, and when your guest is

ready to leave you might go into Betty's room, or call her in from outdoors, for a brief introduction. If she has been prepared in advance, she should be able to manage a handshake or a curtsey, and a "How do you do?"

In regard to a dinner party, the question of readiness is most important. If your child has been able to manage herself easily and well with casual guests staying for dinner, she may be ready for a "fancier" party. Such a dinner is generally long-drawn-out, compared to an ordinary meal, and may have more courses than a small child can eat. If you feel your youngster is ready for it, let her be a member of the party. Call her to the table at the last possible minute. Serve her first, explaining the need for this to your adult guests, if necessary. Make her portions tiny. Excuse her after the main course, call her back for dessert, and excuse her again the moment she has finished.

If she is not ready to dine with your company, feed her in advance. Should you be preparing some very special food, make every effort to serve her the same thing. If this is impossible, don't give her a bowl of dry cereal; prepare something she especially likes so she won't feel left out. Then, unless she is to go to bed before you serve dinner, leave a place for her at the table. For most boys and many girls this can be "standing room"—a space, a small plate, but no chair. If she really wants a chair, when the time comes, she can go get one—a good occupation! Then she can come and go, having a nibble of food if she wants it. Should this seem unreasonable, feed her in advance, arrange for some play situation to occupy her for the duration of dinner, but call her to have dessert at the table with the company.

It is not reasonable to exclude her from the dining room entirely, unless the meal takes place after her bedtime. On the other hand it is not reasonable to expect her to sit through even a family dinner party when she is not ready. One of the compromises outlined can provide a limited but successful experience.

## THE BABY SITTER

You may think of the baby sitter as a kind of specialized servant, rather than as a guest, but your child cannot make that kind of differentiation. Even if she could, it would be better for your child to think of the baby sitter as a visitor—someone who has come especially to see her because she likes her.

Until she was a year-and-a-half or even two, you were able to get any baby sitter. Betty was generally asleep before you went out for the evening. If she did wake up, the baby sitter could change her or give her a bottle, and her needs were met. But suddenly, at two or so, she begins to feel very differently about it. Until your child is five or six, at least, the personality of the baby sitter is of more importance to her than the sitter's maturity, reliability, and other factors which seem important to you. How do you start a new baby sitter?

1. It is best for your child to know her in advance. If she is a stranger, have her call one afternoon (preferably not the same day she will come to sit) and chat with you and Betty for a few minutes. After that, speak about her often, to give Betty the feeling that she is a rather intimate connection, and speak warmly so that the idea of being with her becomes a pleasant one.

2. At least the first time she comes, it is better for you to do

the entire bed-putting routine, but have the sitter be present. In this way she will learn your particular routine, and Betty will associate her with a comfortable situation.

3. Assure the new baby sitter that it is more important for your child to be comfortable and happy than for her to follow a prescribed routine. If she wants the light in the hall left on, or her door open, or to have the sitter stay in her room until she falls asleep—even though she may not ordinarily make such demands—it is better to have the sitter allow these things than to quiet her with threats, scolding or punishment.

4. Encourage Betty to talk about the baby sitter next day. Any fears she has about going to sleep with you away will seem less awesome when discussed in broad daylight, and talking about the sitter may make it easy for her to air the entire experience.

## WHEN GRANDMA COMES TO STAY

It happens to many young families that an older relative comes for an extended, perhaps permanent, visit. This may be, in some ways, a pleasure—but in other ways it is bound to be hard on you. It can be most trying to a young child, and threatening to her growing independence. Several things you can do will protect your child from the difficulties involved.

Although it might seem most convenient to move Grandma in with Betty, this should be done only as a very last resort. If Betty's room must be given over to Grandma, move Betty to a new place if at all possible. Even a sleeping porch or dining room would be preferable to a shared room for your child.

If changes in your child's way of behaving are required—such as quiet during certain times of the day—do not expect her to take on these changes all at once just because you say she must. Children cannot adapt themselves to new conditions by a mere effort of will, as adults do. If there is a quiet time required while Grandma is resting, explain this to Betty—and then make it easy for her to cooperate. Go outdoors with her, the first few times, or go visiting. Perhaps you might arrange your shopping to coincide with Grandma's rest. When you have to be home, make sure that you provide Betty with a quiet occupation that is really fun. In this way many rest periods will pass during which Betty is aware that quiet has been provided, but in which she has made no sacrifice in order to provide it. Before long the idea of the quiet time will be established as a habit.

Or, again, suppose Grandma is so upset about your child's manners that you decide it is worth while to get the youngster to say *please* and *thank you* on every occasion. You might make a chart on which Betty marks a check every time she says *thanks* or *please,* and erases two checks each time she forgets—with a tiny candy to be paid each time she gets up to ten or twenty checks. Good manners are not taught by means of bribes—but a change of manners can be brought about in the guise of a game. Otherwise it will entail constant, nagging reminders, since it is almost as hard for children to change their habits as it is for adults.

One mistake, often made when old folks come to live with a young family, is to allow too much familiarity in the beginning between the old person and the child. When Grandma first comes it is a great novelty and Betty wants to be with her almost all the time. Probably the reverse is also true. After a while, as the novelty wears off, one or both begin to feel a lack of privacy, and hostility begins to replace the pleasant excitement of the early days. It is well to avoid this by establishing at once areas of privacy and times of privacy, and sticking to them pretty firmly.

## THE MOST PERMANENT GUEST — BABY

Undoubtedly the most difficult problems in the life of your preschooler center around the arrival of a new baby. That this can be a threat to her growing independence can be seen very clearly. The older child greets the newcomer only too often by reverting to earlier patterns—bedwetting, thumb sucking, baby-talk, fear of the dark, and so on. This can be explained in many ways.

In a sense, she is trying to be a baby again so that the new baby will not replace her. In a different sense, she *is* a baby again, since the newcomer involves for her a loss of security which produces a loss of maturity. In addition, she unconsciously uses this behavior as a way of competing with the baby for the attention of family and friends.

This does not mean, of course, that when a second child is born the first retrogresses in all ways. The child continues to grow. The retrogression is shown in different areas, and to different degrees, by different children. If your child's loss of maturity shows up in many ways and is evident most of the time, you should look for psychiatric help at once. Caught early, this kind of trouble can be solved with relative ease. But most youngsters will seem less mature, when baby comes, in one or several specific traits, while in general their normal growth continues.

However, there are ways of making the advent of a new baby a cue for increased independence, rather than a touchstone for renewed dependence. The essential demand is that the child is himself well loved and that the newcomer is wholeheartedly welcomed by his parents. Granted this, there are techniques that will help.

## GETTING READY FOR THE NEWCOMER

Several months before the baby is due, your little child should be told about it. She should be told that it is on its way but that it won't arrive for a long, long time. (Remember, even a week is a long, long time for a preschooler; that is why it is suggested that she share the last months of your pregnancy rather than all of them.) She should be told that the baby is inside her mother, and as it grows evident to an observer, the growth should be pointed out to her. If this results in her asking further questions, such as how the baby got to be inside of Mommy, this may also be the time to tell her. Tell her* what she wants to know, but don't go beyond what she asks. Keep it simple.

The baby should be referred to as "our baby." Betty should be told how little and helpless it will be, and that she was once equally little and helpless, but that now she is big and strong and clever. She can be told that sooner or later she will have a brother

---

* See "How to Tell Your Child About Sex," by James L. Hymes, Public Affairs Press.

or sister to play with, but that for years the baby will be too little to play with and will need to be taken care of instead.

If baby equipment is to be bought, she can be in on the shopping. If her old things are to be brought out and spruced up, perhaps she can help with that. In many ways, before baby comes, the child can be helping. In addition, she should know in what ways she will be able to help, after baby comes, and what changes in her own behavior will be required. (For the first six months, incidentally, these may be very few, as the new baby's sleep will not be affected by the older child's noise, and his routines can be established so as not to conflict too much with hers.)

Do not, during your pregnancy or during the first year of the baby's life, try to make Betty independent by means of less cuddling and reassurance. During this time she needs more—together with real recognition of the things she does well on her own level of development.

## HELPING WITH BABY

Betty will enjoy almost every opportunity for helping with the baby. (Of course, little boys like doing this too.) This increases the feeling that it is "our baby" and not "your baby which has taken my place." In addition, this will help her growing independence instead of impairing it.

To start with, like a nurse attending a surgeon, she can hand you safety pins for diapering, powder and towel after baby's bath. However, a way should be made as quickly as possible for her to do part or all of the diapering, part of the bathing or drying. When baby is weaned, the older child can hold the bottle or the cup and help in many ways with the feeding. Pushing a baby carriage or stroller is likely to be more fun than a chore. If Betty is sharing the work with baby (to however small a degree) let her share also in decisions. "Should we give him his orange juice now or at the 10 o'clock feeding?" Or, "Do you think he'll be too warm if we put the extra blanket on?"

Most important, however, is to remember this: However much praise and attention Betty gets for helping with baby, don't let this

become the only area in which she can count on praise and attention. You must make an unrelenting effort to be aware of her as a three-year-old, or a five-year-old, or whatever she may be. Appreciate all of her three-year-old behavior just as you would have if a new baby hadn't come along. This is not as easy to do as it is to say, but it can be done.

Furthermore, you can get your close friends and relatives, all the adults with whom she is in frequent contact, to cooperate. Nothing is more discouraging than to have your erstwhile favorite aunt greet you with, "Hi, Betty, and how is that new baby brother?" When your adult friend, who is Betty's friend, too, comes to visit, try to get her to spend a little time with Betty before she goes in to coo over the baby, and perhaps again afterwards.

Many people find it advantageous to start a child in at nursery school about the time a new baby is expected, so that she will have the opportunity to develop fully at her own age level in an atmosphere not permeated with baby, an atmosphere in which she is important for herself, not merely as the big sister of a newcomer. The final chapter of this book deals at length with ways in which you can help your preschooler get a good start at school, but a word here is in order if you plan to send Betty to nursery school at about this time.

To go off to a new and difficult situation out of the home, at the same time that home itself is presenting a new and difficult situation, seems like a lot to ask of a little child. Further, if every child suspects to some degree that the new baby is supplanting her, what better proof could she ask than the fact that she is being daily sent away at the same time that the new one is invited in? What a poor way in which to start one's school life, feeling that school is a place of exile rather than a desirable place to go! A better way is to get Betty started at nursery school well before the new baby is born. The baby's arrival will not interrupt the continuity of this phase of Betty's life.

# 4. Billy's Own Social Life

Little mention has been made so far of your preschooler's own social life. He should have ample opportunity to visit and to have visitors among people *of his own age*. A program of frequent, casual, easy-going intervisitation can be of great value in a child's life, especially in the life of an only child. If your community has no nursery school or if for other reasons you cannot avail yourself of one, this visiting program can be absolutely essential.

A few children at two, and most children by the time they are well into their third year, are ready to start calling on friends. In a suburb or a small town, where neighborhood children play together and can move independently up and down the street, this will probably start automatically.

You see Billy playing on the lawn with Suzie from the red house on the corner, and it's easy to invite them both in for a glass of milk and a piece of cake. If they have been out for a long time, you can suggest that they come in and play for a while in Billy's room. Stay with them, as long as necessary to make Suzie feel comfortable. When you leave the room, if it seems desirable, tell Suzie where you will be and that if she calls you will come. Perhaps she will feel more at ease if you phone Suzie's mother to tell her where she is, and you let Suzie say hello, too. Make these first visits brief. End them before Suzie becomes worried about being away from home, and before Billy becomes concerned about sharing his possessions (and his mother) with her.

Perhaps Suzie's mother will start this process rolling. If not, you begin. When you have once done so, she will probably go along with you. Having visited together at your house, the children will quickly decide that they want to visit at hers.

Serve snacks to your child's guests on several occasions before inviting them for lunch or supper. This will get them used to the idea of eating in your house under the easiest circumstances. Furthermore, snacks usually consist of things children like to eat rather than those which grownups think are good for them. This makes it easier, too.

Avoid using Billy's visit to Suzie as an opportunity for you to go shopping—at least, until there have been many such visits and you know beyond doubt that he is comfortable and safe there. Don't, in any case, send him off to Suzie's with the idea that you will be home, and then go out. If his visit should end early, or if he and Suzie should come over to pick up a toy, he will be horrified to find you gone.

If his initial visits at Suzie's house seem to go on too long, go and call for him. You can easily explain to Suzie's mother, should it seem necessary, the advantage of short visits until both children are well used to the visiting situation and fully at home in each other's house.

## JUVENILE "DATES"

For city people, or for anyone living in a neighborhood without appropriate small fry neighbors, the social life of your preschooler will take a lot of doing on your part. The fact that arranging visits is difficult for you, though, does not mean it should be avoided. The same circumstances which make it so, make it all the more necessary for your child.

You will probably have to arrange a "date" in advance, take your child to his friend's house, stay there until it is time for him to leave, and then take him home. On the return visit, you will likewise need to entertain the friend's mother while the children play. If the children are good friends and get along well, it may not take more than one such exchange. After that Billy will not need to have you in the house in order for him to be comfortable.

If the children attend nursery school, you will probably want to make the arrangement that many schools foster: When a child is to visit another, after school, the mother of the host is responsible for getting them both to her house, and the mother of the guest is responsible for picking up her child at the conclusion of the "date."

As explained in the section above, these visits should be short and should not include meals until the situation has grown quite familiar. This makes it even more arduous for you, no doubt, to have to take Billy all the way to Joey's house and then have to call for him again when barely an hour has gone by. But careful handling of these little visits give him a chance to develop the sense of ease which will make more independent visiting a simple next step.

Do not be concerned if your youngster is not ready for such visits as soon as you might wish. You can still arrange for him to meet his friends in the park or another public place. And don't keep him from having guests just because he isn't ready to *be* one. Children don't worry about reciprocating, and the enjoyment of having friends at his house will serve to hasten his wish to return the calls.

## THE BUSINESS OF SHARING

As your child begins to visit back and forth with his friends, he will be squarely faced with the business of sharing playthings. The ability to share is not merely a step toward independence, but evidence of independence achieved. It doesn't necessarily come early, and its growth does not generally follow a regular pattern. The child who can share everything at three years may be unable to share at five or six. The child who shares today with Cousin Jack may not wish to share tomorrow with Cousin Jim. The child who can easily share his toy truck and his teddy bear may refuse to share his boat or his puppet. He may share his favorite possession and decline to share some toy that he never actually plays with.

These facts are true, by and large, of all children. Do not expect your child to make steady, even progress. It is important to have this bit of knowledge to save you from disappointment, and keep you from blaming your youngster where he is not blameworthy.

"A child must know how to own before he can begin to share," said a well-known educator. That means he must feel completely secure in his ownership. If you deprive him of certain toys as a punishment, or take away a toy which you feel he has abused, or lend his toys to other children against his wishes, you then make him less secure in his feeling of ownership and consequently less able to share.

It is a good idea, when he goes on initial visits, to have him take a plaything along. Then he will have something to use if his friend is unready to share. It also provides a possibility of exchange sharing. The friend may be willing to let him use his toys, while he plays with the toy that Billy has brought along.

When another child is coming to visit, you might have ready early in the game two inexpensive identical toys for them to play with. These may be gifts, but better yet they can be *yours,* remaining yours when the visit is over.

It is also helpful, before a visitor comes, to talk with Billy about his plans, particularly what his friend will be able to play with. If he offers only one or two items, you might suggest others until you have a reasonable list for the guest to choose from. Remind him of this agreement just before his friend arrives. But don't be shocked if it doesn't work. A child—like anyone else—reserves the right to change his mind. Best plan is for you to be ready and suggest a suitable alternative activity that does not involve the sharing of your youngster's possessions.

There are certain standard items, too, which don't especially involve sharing as they are multiple rather than single by nature—building blocks, costume material, sand box, finger painting equipment, materials for sewing, etc. And there are others so inexpensive that you can easily keep an extra one on hand so there will always be two available—bubble pipes, sets of stringing beads, boxes of crayons.

Difficult as learning to share may be, it is obviously of first importance. A great advantage of nursery schools is that they ease this process along. But, without nursery school, and especially in the case of an only child, frequent visiting with other children will give your child the opportunity to learn.

## BIRTHDAY PARTIES

Birthday parties can be fun for everyone, or they can be trying for the children and murderous for the parents. In any case, they are inevitable. Three rules may help you make these occasions successful instead of an ordeal.

Rule 1. Make them brief. An hour, nearly half of which may be spent at the table, is plenty for a third or fourth birthday. An hour and a half is a good length for a fifth or sixth birthday, with two hours reasonable when your child turns seven, eight or nine.

Rule 2. Make them small. Invite at least two fewer children than you feel you can handle. If you have had no previous experience, it can be astonishingly hard to keep the youngsters occupied and happy. For a two-year-old no guests at all are necessary. A small family party with favors, ice cream and cake, and the singing of "Happy Birthday to You" will be just right. You might make an exception, of course, to include a constant companion, the child next door with whom your youngster plays every day, a cousin whom he sees very frequently, or a favorite adult friend.

The size of the party and how long it may pleasurably last depend in part on where you live, the season and the weather. If much or all of the proceedings can take place outdoors, you can handle more children and keep them happy longer.

Rule 3. Plan the party with your child. Let him make up the guest list with you. Let him choose the flavor of the ice cream, the cake, the icing. Work with him on planning the games. Incidentally, it's a good idea *not* to play only games in which a winner is chosen. Preschoolers like to sing together, with a grownup leading, or to do rhythm play, take turns imitating animals, draw or paint, and many other non-competitive activities. And it certainly is unnecessary to have prizes for winners. If there are games of that kind, let the winner have the right to announce the next game, or to serve the ice cream!

It is a very good idea for you and your child to *make* the party hats, candy baskets, and other decorations. If he has done any baking, let him bake his own birthday cake (but you must decorate it, so it will be a surprise). This may be more fun for him than the party itself will be. In any case, it will give him a head start toward feeling that the party is *his* and that he can manage it.

# 5. Suzie and Those Men in White

Countless children develop a fear of doctors during their pre-school years. This can cause the children (and their parents) unnecessary agony, and even though the fear eventually disappears, there is often a carry-over into adult life. Furthermore, this fear spills over to include dentists, nurses, opticians, even barbers. Of all these people, the doctor comes first in your child's life, both chronologically and in order of importance.

From birth your child has been seeing a doctor. For the first year or so, she did not react any differently toward him than toward any other person. Then suddenly going to the doctor may become a terrifying ordeal. What can be done about it?

The first step is to choose a doctor who is compatible to your own particular child. If your child doesn't react well to your regular family doctor, why not choose a different doctor just for her? If you live in a town big enough to have pediatricians, don't be embarrassed to "shop around" until you find one who suits your child. The difference between a good doctor and the best doctor (as though there were any way of judging!) is less important, during childhood, than to find one who can make Suzie smile.

Injections probably cause more bad relations between children and doctors than anything else. Many a pediatrician has someone else give shots, a younger associate or simply another doctor who shares his office. In child health clinics shots are generally given by a nurse in one room, while the doctor holds forth in a different room. These helpful situations are not easy to come by, however.

You will need to take steps, in cooperation with your doctor, to prevent injections from damaging his relations with your child.

When going to a new doctor, or to your old doctor at a time when your child has just become aware of him and his function, do not have any shots. Since most shots are routine, this can be arranged (in advance) very easily. Better yet, have two shot-less visits, to allow a friendship to develop that can withstand the puncture of a needle.

If possible, go for shots separately from ordinary visits throughout Suzie's childhood. Then at times you will tell her, "We have to go to Dr. Jones for shots today." Even though this is an upsetting idea, it is better not to conceal the truth. And, other times, you can say, "We have to go to Dr. Jones today for a check-up. No shots!"

If you cannot make separate visits, it is probably better to have the injection first thing. If it is put off until the end of the visit, the child will spend the entire time dreading it. Get it over with at the start and let the rest of the visit be a comfortable one. Be sure to make all these arrangements in advance. You'd be in a bad spot if you said, "No shots," and the doctor didn't know it. Many doctors make a practice of popping a lollypop into a child's mouth the instant a shot is over. If your doctor doesn't, or if you are not sure, take one in your pocketbook for the purpose.

Try to arrange time appointments, rather than going just "during office hours" when everyone piles up in the waiting room and takes his turn. Waiting to go in will give Suzie an unnecessary opportunity to see other children and build up her dread. In any case, be sure to take playthings or a new book to read to her while waiting, unless you see a pediatrician who has plenty of play equipment in the waiting room. Keeping busy will take the sting out of the waiting period.

Tell your child the truth and encourage your doctor to do the same. If you tell her that stitches don't hurt, why should she believes you another time when you explain that fluoroscopes or tongue depressors or stethoscopes don't hurt? Say, "This shot will hurt, but only for a minute. You know that!"

## THE HOSPITAL

The chance of Suzie's being hospitalized during her preschool years is fairly slight, compared to what it would have been twenty years ago. At that time tonsillectomies were considered inevitable, and the question was *when* rather than *whether*. Today doctors are less prone to remove tonsils, and parents are more aware of how difficult an emotional experience is involved in early hospitalization. The disadvantage is that now a first hospitalization is likely to result from an emergency, with little opportunity for advance preparation.

Nevertheless, preparation is urgent. If you can plan it for a week in advance, do so. But even if it has to take place while driving from the scene of an accident to the hospital, do all that you can.

Explain what will happen in as much detail as possible: about getting into bed, about the ride to the operating room, about anesthesia, about when she will wake up, and when she will go home. Tell her especially when you will be there (and make it every possible moment) and about the nurses who will give her anything she needs when you cannot be present. Perhaps you can play-act being a nurse, and in that role be a little more considerate than usual, so as to give her a positive picture. If she knows a nurse—and likes her—you can say that the nurses who take care of her will be just as nice and kind as So-and-so.

Make sure that she understands about the use of anesthetics— that she will be asleep, and when she wakes up the operation will be all over. That it will be a sound sleep, and no matter what the doctor does she won't wake up during it and she won't feel anything. That it will be a brief sleep ("about as long as it takes you to drink your glass of milk"), since she may secretly fear that she won't ever wake up again.

Most important, however, is for you to arrange to spend as much time with her as the hospital regulations allow (or as they can be stretched to allow). Not enough nurses have the inclination or the training to deal with children's emotional needs, and even should the nurses have the ability to keep your child interested and happy, they probably will not have the time.

Be sure to send along a book and a toy or two, to help occupy her hours and to give her something familiar as a talisman in strange surroundings. Take something along at each visit. A gift of something new is nice, but sometimes one of her own playthings from home is more effective. And don't forget the ice cream which has been for so many children (especially those having their tonsils removed) the only memorable moment in their hospital stay.

## FIRST ILLNESS AND CONVALESCENCE

There may be many times when Suzie feels slightly under the weather or has a mild cold, necessitating more rest and quieter occupations than usual. But special efforts on your part are needed when she first contracts a real illness which will keep her in bed for more than a day.

As soon as the doctor has made a diagnosis, tell her what is wrong and what it will entail. It is easier for children, as for adults, to face known hardships than vague ones. Say, "Dr. Brown said you have chicken pox and that you'll have to stay in bed for at least three or four days. Even after that you won't be able to go outdoors for a few days, though you'll be out of bed." In mentioning how long she will be confined, state the maximum probable time. It will be easier, later on, to say, "You can get up a day sooner than we thought," than to have to admit, "Yes, the four days are up, but Dr. Brown wants you to have an extra day or two in bed."

If there is to be a regular program of medication, explain this as well. Any other special arrangements, such as sleeping after lunch (though she may have given up sleeping at nap time, as a normal thing), should be mentioned now. At the same time, you can plan with her those parts of the experience that will be pleasantly novel. Tell her about having meals in bed, perhaps ice cream every day following her nap and special things like cambric tea or lots of lemonade. Tell her of a few new occupations you will provide, and tell her, too, what *your* schedule will be. Then you and she can plan better for the hours she will spend alone or with others, and those when she will have your company. This should help to prevent her from struggling to keep you constantly by her side, and enable you to get away at intervals to do your essential household work.

Since she will want you with her more times than you can manage, it pays to plan to do things in her room that you might ordinarily do elsewhere. When you bring her luncheon tray to her bed, why not bring another tray with your own lunch on it? Some household chores, like ironing or preparing vegetables for cooking, can be done in her room without too much extra work. And, of course, this is the time to give up some of the routine tasks and catch up on your sewing, mending, knitting and crocheting, all of which you can do in the sickroom.

Your child has to know how serious the illness is, or the staying in bed and other inconveniences don't make sense. On the other hand, don't give her the feeling that her life is in danger or her future health threatened. Ideally, a child should take good health for granted, with just enough awareness to support the need for a well-rounded diet, warm enough clothes, and following the doctor's orders when sick.

During convalescence the strain will be much greater. Often a child feels entirely well before doctor or mother is ready to let her resume normal activities. During this period you must be more imaginative than ever (and sacrificing of your own convenience) to keep her so busy that she won't spend her days in frustrating captivity.

It is often wise, with the doctor's approval, to establish a routine of calisthenics or some other physical exercise for limited periods. This may take the edge off her need for physical activity, but it can easily be controlled to prevent fatigue, overheating, or undue excitement.

Most children can be expected to go through two to six childhood diseases (not to speak of such incidentals as broken arms) between birth and adolescence. Helping her cope with the first such situation may make any future ones easier on her and on you.

## THE DENTIST

Even if your child doesn't need dental work during her preschool years, it is important for her to have a periodic dental checkup. The first visit to a dentist's office is the important one. The first time, the dentist should do no more than inspect your preschooler's teeth. This will help her establish a secure feeling in the dental chair against the time when she will need dental work in later childhood.

Perhaps before your preschooler goes to the dentist for this kind of checkup, you will be able to build up to it gradually. For instance, take Suzie along when you go to the dentist, especially when you are going for tooth cleaning or a trivial cavity, anything which will not have you writhing in the chair. Let her watch what the dentist is doing. Ask the dentist to explain the various tools, especially those that can't possibly hurt, like the mirrors and the saliva suction apparatus.

When your child is used to the total situation and has friendly feelings toward the dentist, you can suggest that she might like to "go up and down" in the dentist's chair—without having the dentist look at her teeth. Or, suggest that she show the dentist her teeth without getting into the chair. Having plenty of time, you don't need to ask her to take both those steps at once.

Many dentists who work with children make a practice of checking with parents before doing any work. If you are not sure, you might tactfully inquire if he works this way. There is a big difference between his, "It might pay to fill that baby tooth," and his, "That tooth has to be filled." In any case, if there is work to be done, ask the dentist not to do it the first time Suzie manages to get into the chair and open her mouth for him. Let her do that on a couple of occasions without any unpleasant results. Then, when the time comes, the dentist can explain what will happen and why. By that time, she should be able to take it.

Incidentally, if Suzie's beginning with the dentist is complicated by negative feelings about doctors, you might try to get on first name terms with your dentist. Saying, "We have to go see Dan (or Uncle Dan)," would be more reassuring than, "We have to go to Dr. Carson's."

# EYEGLASSES

Preschoolers who have to wear glasses are somewhat handicapped, but less so than adults generally think. Most people nowadays accept glasses realistically, but some grownups are so surprised to find a very little child with glasses that they tend to say, "Oh, isn't it a shame." Actually, it's easier for a preschooler to start than for a school-age child. If a parent or other loved person, even another child, wears glasses, a preschooler often *wants* them.

Once a child is seven or eight she is likely to feel that the glasses ruin her appearance, if she is a girl, or that they impair his masculinity if he is a boy. Your preschooler is handicapped (a) by you, if you put too much pressure on her to wear the glasses and not to let them get broken, and (b) by other adults, if they insist on pitying her.

When Suzie's eyes are measured for glasses, you had better give her an advance picture of what will happen. The apparatus can be quite frightening to a small child, but with advance notice it is likely to be amusing instead. Explain about the great heavy eyeglass testing frames which will make her look like a Man From Mars, and how different lenses will be dropped in, like coins into a slot, until the right combination for her eyes is discovered.

As far as the glasses themselves are concerned, the doctor may tell you that she should wear them all the time. In fact, this is most common in the case of very young children. Don't be surprised if it takes a month or two to accomplish this. For a long time she will forget to put her glasses back on nearly every time she removes them. Give her time. As she gradually comes to depend on the convenience of better vision, she will start wearing the glasses with increased regularity.

The other problem is your own concern about her possibly breaking the glasses. Obviously glasses are expensive, and replacing them is inconvenient as well. But she will easily realize how breakable they are, and the less you call her attention to it, the less the glasses will hamper her independence. It may be some comfort to realize that children's glasses, like children's shoes, are quickly outgrown. When Suzie breaks her glasses you will probably discover that it was time for the lenses to be changed anyway, or that the frames had become too small. The fact is, she can break a pair of glasses a year, more or less, without their costing you much more than if she never broke any at all.

As far as your adult acquaintances are concerned, you might tell them (especially before they see Suzie in her new glasses for the first time) that you would appreciate their cooperation. Ask

them to say she looks well in them, and not to say "What a pity"—
or, better yet, not to mention them at all, as if they were of no
consequence, unless Suzie calls the matter to their attention herself.

## HIPPITY HOP TO THE BARBER SHOP

Though a haircut has nothing to do with health, to your little
boy the barber may seem very much like a doctor or dentist. Like
them, he wears white. Like them, he demands that Billy sit motionless for a longer period than any preschooler is inclined to sit
motionless. His chair is certainly first cousin to the dentist's chair.
If Billy has any fear of the medical profession, he is likely to
approach the barber shop with the same feelings.

The simple solution is for you to cut his hair yourself, and
any parent can do a perfectly satisfactory job at least for a few
years. At the same time, let him accompany his father to the
barber shop as often as possible, without having the child's hair
cut. Do this especially at a time when you feel that he must soon
start going himself. During this period, you might also play-act
being a barber and encourage him to act the customer. Perhaps
you can even get a tip out of him for your trouble!

Just before he goes for his first professional haircut, remind
him there are certain discomforts, but that men put up with them
and he can do the same. However, make it clear that if the sheet
is too tight at his neck or the clippings too itchy on his face, a
firm, non-querulous request will undoubtedly bring results.

# 6. Johnnie Steps into the Glamorous World

Many special events, which adults do sheerly for pleasure, are not pleasures but trying events for the preschooler (and the parent) until he gets the hang of them. Eating out in restaurants, going to movies, theatre or concerts, visiting amusement parks and county fairs, even museums and zoos—these are things you do for your child's pleasure, and it is disappointing to discover that he would have been far better pleased with a walk around the block and an ice cream cone. Sometimes we have to learn our pleasures as well as our duties, and you can help your child learn to manage and enjoy the more glamorous aspects of the world he lives in.

The question of readiness may not enter into these activities— they are the extra-special things. An opportunity arises sometimes and you go ahead! It is more important to make proper selection of activities (what kind of restaurant? which movie?) and prepare your youngster a little bit in advance.

It is also important that your expectations of Johnnie's behavior and enjoyment be geared low enough so that you won't be disappointed in him. This matter of expectation is vital in all aspects of child-parent relations. If you take your two-year-old for his first trip to the zoo and he is enthralled by the pigeons in front of the elephant cage but barely notices the elephants, he may note your chagrin and feel that he has failed. If pigeons delight him and elephants are a bore, why not be pleased with his delight?

# GOING TO A RESTAURANT

For first trips to a restaurant it is well to choose an eating place that caters to "family trade" and is used to having children. Such a place is likely to have high-chairs, small size dinners for children, and waiters who are patient. Most important, you need not be too embarrassed if Johnnie makes a little noise or spills a glass of water, since you will be aware that these occurrences are not without precedent.

If Johnnie is two, three or four, you will probably order for him. In this case, let him know in advance. If he thinks he is going to select from the menu and then learns that you are doing the choosing, his dining out will be off to a bad start. At four, five or six, he may be able to make his own selection, with some help from you. Make it clear beforehand what the nature of that help will be—seeing to it that he orders something he probably will like, that he doesn't order more than he probably will eat.

Many parents don't order separately for little children, but give them food from their own plates. If you plan to do this, make sure the waiter sets a place for your child so he has his own silver, napkin, water, and so forth. It is also nice to order *a la carte* for him any dish which cannot readily be divided. He might well have his own fruit cup or bowl of soup, though he is to share the main course with you. Unless one of the adults plans not to eat dessert, order an individual dessert for Johnnie. And here you can certainly let him choose. This is likely to be the high spot of the entire experience for him.

Just as when you dine out at the home of friends, the hardest part of the restaurant meal for Johnnie is having to sit still for a longer time than he wants. Why not pass some of the time between the placing of your order and the arrival of the food with a trip to the washroom, even if he washed up before leaving home? Between the main course and dessert is likely to be another difficult time. Try to find something for him to do away from the table during this interval. Maybe you can induce the waiter to take him out to see the big restaurant kitchen. Perhaps he can take a little walk outside with an adult, or go to your car if it is parked nearby, or go visit with the cashier, or simply explore the restaurant, keeping out of the way of the waiters. Or, if he cannot leave the table, you can play pencil and paper games with him.

The third waiting period that is hard on Johnnie is after dessert when the adults are lingering over coffee. This can go on for quite a while—in Johnnie's mind, for *years*. The best way around this is to sacrifice your own pleasure a little and don't do it. Drink up your coffee, get your check, and get going!

Don't expect Johnnie to be silent as a little grownup. ("Children should be seen but not heard" is an outdated proverb.) Don't expect him to eat more than he eats at home; he might, but he is more likely to eat next to nothing. And don't expect him to glow with pleasure over this unique experience. The fact that it was fun may occur to him only in retrospect, on talking it over the next day.

## THE DARKENED HALL

Going to a theatre, whether for a play, a movie, a concert or a dance recital, is as exciting for your preschooler as it is for you. It also involves the very trying necessity of sitting absolutely still and keeping absolutely silent for a long time. (Television viewing is no preparation for this.) The very excitement of going to the theatre, of the darkened hall and the anticipation of the performance, makes it even harder for your preschooler to be quiet, since a child's natural response to excitement is to run, jump and shout. For these reasons it is well to think twice before taking Johnnie to a theatre, and then only do so if you are sure the performance will compel his attention.

Most movies that are made for children or recommended for children tend to include episodes that are terrifying to a preschooler. After all, the producer of a children's picture has to count on appealing to the ten-year-old, the fourteen-year-old and a lot of adults, as well as to the very young. He accomplishes this by throwing in violence, suspense, romance, or all three. You will have to decide whether the valuable parts of the picture are sufficiently worth-while to compensate for these elements. If you decide yes, then tell your children several times over to expect the frightening episodes, before you go, and reassure him while they are taking place.

Legitimate plays suitable for Johnnie are few and far between. If they are put on by a professional "children's theatre" group, they may have the same kind of imperfection as in the case of children's movies. Being more lifelike than motion pictures, they are apt to be even more terrifying. But again, if the total play is worth Johnnie's time, you can help him through the more scary sections. Plays put on by school-age children are likely to make better fare for preschoolers. The comparative informality of the situation is easier for Johnnie to take, and if the cast contains brothers or sisters or children he recognizes, he'll be delighted.

Performances of instrumental music are rarely right for preschoolers, even though Johnnie may enjoy listening to your records at home. But a recital of folk songs, or a dance recital of almost any kind, will appeal to him from beginning to end. Many folk singers invite audience participation, and even those who don't, tend to make the audience feel personally involved. This is a very good situation for a child's first visits to the theatre.

Explain thoroughly in advance about the darkness of the theatre, or Johnnie may be upset by it. Roll up his and your overcoats for him to sit on, and allow him to change as often as he wishes from his own seat, to your lap, to standing up in front of his seat. This small amount of physical activity may make all the difference in the world.

## ON THE MIDWAY

Taking Johnnie to an amusement park, county fair, or any similar large-scale entertainment requires discretion. By all means go, but limit the time you stay and the number of attractions you plan to take in on any one visit. Be sure to include some restful activities, such as a picnic lunch or a swim.

Nowadays there is almost always a special area with "rides" scaled down to preschool size. If "rides" are in order, better stick to "Kiddy Land." They don't go too fast and won't result in fear or sickness. There are a few adult "rides" which may be suitable for little ones, however. A big (not too fast) merry-go-round is usually fine even for a three-year-old. A ferris wheel with caged-in cars, if you go with him and hold him tight, will probably be the biggest thrill at the fair for Johnnie. Aside from the excitement of the ride, there is also the pleasant chance to be up in the air where it is cool and quiet, and look down on the hubbub below. Another possibility, as long as one parent accompanies him, is the dodge 'em rink with the little electric cars you can steer yourself. (Johnnie's being accustomed to riding in the family car is enough preparation for this.)

At a county fair you will probably find that Johnnie will want to watch the farm animals on display for a longer time than you do. On the other hand, don't expect him to get much out of displays of prize squash, pickled watermelon rind, or handmade quilts. He is your guest, so why not go where he wants and pass up the things he finds dull? Sometimes Mother and Dad can take turns getting Johnnie to the things he enjoys while the other pursues personal interests.

Two warnings. Johnnie will want to eat a dozen odd things, mostly sweets. Let him. Unless you suggest it, he wouldn't dream of getting sick to his stomach. This is one of the joys of a fair. The other warning is in regard to fireworks. If there is going to be a display, explain exactly how loud and how bright the fireworks will be, or his pleasure in it will be modified by an initial reaction of terror!

## CONTRADICTIONS AT THE FAIR

One aspect of a county fair is extremely confusing to children. Adults have either learned to see past this confusion, or else they have been so long confused that they are no longer aware of it. The confusion is between the educational and the commercial, between strict truth and wild exaggeration. A fair is one place where the contradiction can be seen so clearly as to be comprehensible to a preschool child.

Here is a Jersey cow with a blue ribbon acclaiming it to be the best Jersey at the fair. Nearby is a sideshow which the barker is touting as the best in the world. How is a child to realize that one of these is close to literal truth, while the other makes no serious pretense of being true at all? Here is a booth showing the work of 4-H youngsters who have competed by means of hard work and real skill; next to it is a booth where you are asked to compete by the hazard of a turning wheel for a worthless prize. Do you wonder at the child's confusion of values?

You cannot solve this dilemma for your preschooler, but you can move a little in that direction by informing him in advance that there are two aspects to the fair. One is concerned with arts, crafts, husbandry and domestic science. The other is carnival—it's fun but the kind of fun that fools you or depends on chance. Remind him, as you go about the fair, of the difference. Perhaps if he is as old as five or six he will be able to point out himself which category the various attractions fall in.

## IN THE MUSEUM

Almost every city or good-sized town has a museum of some kind, ranging in size from New York's Museum of Natural History to an old house maintained by the local Historical Society. These are fine places for Johnnie to visit, as long as he goes there with a purpose, rather than as a way to fill an afternoon. His first museum visits may well set the tone for his lifetime reaction to such places. Will museums be exciting to him or will they always represent boredom and fatigue? Largely, it is up to you.

First trips to a museum should be extremely brief. Take him when something has come up in his books or conversation that can be better understood with the help of a museum exhibit. Perhaps you will have been reading to him about pioneer life. He finds the muzzle-loading rifle or the ox yoke hard to visualize. After talking about them, give him a chance to see them at the museum. Thus the museum will become, right from the start, a useful institution that can help him solve his problems.

But *don't* decide that as long as he's going he might as well spend the day there. If, while going to or from the one exhibit you are planning to see, the prehistoric animal relics, for example, strike his fancy—don't decide to investigate them then and there. Tell him you'll come another time to see it. Then he will leave the museum with a spark kindled toward a second visit. And he will leave it without feeling that his legs have turned to rubber.

Before going back to see the display which intrigued him, give him some information about that situation. Get a book on the subject from a bookstore or library (one on his age level) and read it to him. Then return to the museum another day for another experience that will make sense to Johnnie.

## AT THE NEARBY ZOO

A trip to the zoo is most often planned specifically for Johnnie's pleasure. You aren't personally very interested in going, but for his sake you'll submit to it. How disappointing it is then, to find that while you become quite absorbed in the kangaroos and gorillas, Johnnie's main interest turns out to be the desire for peanuts or a balloon. Why should this be? And can it be prevented?

Like a museum, a zoo is too big and too varied to be taken in on one day. The distances you have to walk are in themselves an obstacle to Johnnie's interest. And his mind cannot possibly cope with all the animals, birds and reptiles that are on display.

If you live in or near a town with a zoo, the best plan is to go only to see a small group of animals on one trip, selecting animals in which he is already interested. So many children's books deal with animals that this situation will arise often enough. Read about them, talk about them, then go see them. When you come home you may find that having seen the creatures he now has new questions to ask.

At best, knowledge is not an end product but a touchstone in the search for further knowledge. A book about bears that he has read may send you both to the zoo to see some. The chance to observe them may send you home with curiosity about why polar bears are white while others are black and brown, why there are no more bears (or why there still are bears) in your part of the state, or whether some bears are really herbivorous while others live exclusively on meat.

Under these circumstances, you would merely dilute his interest and distract him from the pursuit of knowledge by stopping to see monkeys and alligators on the way to the bear cages, and lions and anteaters on the way back. As explained in the description of museum trips, above, the glimpses he gets of other animals will assure his desire to return to the zoo shortly. A book about bears may have caused you to go and see some at the zoo; the sight of tigers in passing may cause you to get a book about them when you get home, preparatory to a second zoo trip for a real look at them.

The zoo, at best, can be a place where you can miraculously get to see the strange wild animal about which Johnnie has genuine curiosity, rather than a place to browse about among hundreds of species. Johnnie may have the energy to see all the cages, but in retrospect he will remember only his (or your) tired feet.

## AT THE DISTANT ZOO

If you live where there is no zoo and you get a chance to see one only on a rare visit to another city, you will be tempted to have Johnnie see every last beast. You will say, "That is all very well for people who live nearby, but if Johnnie doesn't see it all now he may not have another opportunity for years and years."

It is still better for him to see only enough so that a vivid impression stays with him, than to see it all and have it blur together in his mind. Under these circumstances, however, you would naturally try to take in more than otherwise, but set up limits in advance. Talk over with Johnnie, in advance, what is offered, and make up a list of what he really wants to see. High on most preschoolers' lists are monkeys, elephants, seals, giraffes, tigers and lions. Birds, reptiles and small mammals usually come last. Make the list reasonable in length. Then if he decides that he really can't pass up the kangaroo house, which is not on the list, you can ask him to substitute it for something that is.

Remember, under these circumstances, that a zoo is also a park. Plan to see some animals in the morning. Then find a nice grassy place where you can have your picnic lunch and a rest. Perhaps for rest hour you will have brought along a book about animals, or some bread crumbs to feed the pigeons. After rest, it would be a good idea to let him have some running around or climbing before continuing the tour. The kind of fatigue that zoos produce is due to slow walking; running and jumping is just as good to overcome it as a chance to sit down. Then look at some more animals, with a break later on for ice cream or popcorn.

In this way, though you won't have seen the whole zoo, Johnnie will have had a wonderful day and one which he will be able to remember.

## FEAR IN THE ZOO

There are not many things in a zoo which frighten children, but it is well to prepare your little one before going. Make sure Johnnie understands that the animals are enclosed and cannot get out. Especially in the case of modern zoos which substitute moats for bars, this should have advance explanation and additional reassurance during the visit.

Where animals are kept indoors it is especially important to warn Johnnie that tremendous roars and shrieks may occur, especially among the lions, tigers, apes and monkeys. Children are much more likely to be frightened by the sudden and unexpected, so the occasional surprising scream of a small monkey may be much more terrifying than the tremendous but expected bellow of a great lion.

Also, if the animals are indoors, warn Johnnie in advance about the "funny" smell. Many children find it hard to take without nausea, but it is easier for a youngster if he is told about it in advance, instead of merely stumbling into it.

# 7. Judy and Shopping

From the time she was too little to remember, Judy has gone with you to different stores. But between the ages of two and six, new problems arise. Now she is aware. She realizes that certain demands are made on her. She has certain desires about what shall be bought and how long a shopping expedition may go on. She is no longer something you merely take along when you go shopping, but a full-fledged member of the expedition.

Several general rules apply to almost all shopping trips. You can help by explaining in advance where you are going and about how long it will take. You can help by telling her what you intend to buy and better yet by giving her some choices, too. A child who might find a trip to the supermarket boring can discover that it is exciting when it includes the box of Crunchies which she herself requested.

In many situations it is important to tell her before you set out what the limits on her choice will be; or that she will have no choice, if that is to be the case. It is very disappointing for a child to be told that she is to select a new pair of shoes, only to discover that the patent leather pumps she wants are out of the question since everyday play shoes are the matter in hand. More on this later.

It is a good idea, when shopping with a small child in a store where you might be detained, to note the windows of adjacent stores for items of interest. Then it will often be possible, when the moment of restlessness approaches, to tell Judy to wait outside and that she can look in the window of the toy shop next door. If you go in your car, check out when she gets restless; then leave her in the car and return for the balance of your shopping.

# SHOPPING FOR FOOD

A written shopping list may not be necessary for you, but it helps make a trip to the supermarket understandable to your child. It is especially valuable if it is arranged in categories. Then you can say, we are going to get this and that at the meat counter, cans of this fruit and that vegetable, paper towels and paper napkins, so many pounds of sugar, so many of flour. You can even construct your list in the same order in which the items will be found in the store.

While writing the list, find some items about which the child's advice can be asked—but only if you are willing to accept it. In addition, why not leave something open for her to choose for you in the store itself? You might say, "Let's just write down pudding and you can choose which kind of pudding when you see them in the store."

If you have to take a young preschooler along during a crowded time, it's best to keep her in the basket seat. Getting lost in the crowds can be really terrifying. Try a box of animal crackers or cheese tidbits, to keep her busy, or open a box of dry cereal and give her handfuls.

Try to go to the supermarket at an off hour, when it is not too crowded. Few children past the age of two will be happy tied into the jump seat on the shopping basket for more than a little while at a time. They will want to spend part of the time pushing the basket themselves, part riding with their feet on the chassis and holding the upper edge with their hands, part walking about the store on their own. Furthermore, taking the items you point out from the shelves and putting them in the basket for you is an excellent activity for any preschooler. It gives Judy the feeling of cooperating in a joint venture, as well as some physical exercise to prevent monotony.

# NEW FOODS

An incidental advantage to shopping trips when the store is not crowded and you don't feel rushed, is the opportunity to introduce Judy to new foods. Show her a package and tell her what its contents are like when prepared for the table. Most likely she will ask you to buy it, and she will be predisposed to like it when it is served. Even better are the times when she discovers something herself and asks for it.

You can steer her toward the stall where fresh Brussels sprouts are on display, for example, and she'll be a rare child if she doesn't decide that she wants some. (She still may not like the food when it's cooked, but she will be more inclined to than not.) Even when she does not ask you to buy an item, your showing it to her and telling her about it as you put it in the basket will give her some feeling of complicity in its purchase. This is far more agreeable to most preschoolers than to have a new dish arrive unannounced on the table.

If your community affords the variety, it is especially interesting for your preschooler to go to individual food stores, on occasion, instead of the supermarket. The butcher shop where the actual butchering can be seen, the greengrocer with his great variety of vegetables, a fish market with sea creatures attractively displayed on shaved ice, the bakery with its warm and luscious smells (and the possibility of a gift cookie for Judy)—all these are adventures in themselves. They also make easier the first time Judy tries new foods and the first time she goes to the store alone. In these shops she cannot get lost, she is less likely to forget her errand, and she can quickly find what she needs.

## PLAYING STORE

If trips to the store seem rather overwhelming for your child, you can help her along by showing her how to play store. In the summer she can use all kinds of weeds and seeds, plantain leaves for spinach, maple leaves for lettuce, buttercups for butter, different hay seeds for sugar, coffee, flour. In the winter, give her empty food boxes and tin cans which have been opened in such a way as to look intact. Another possibility, good at any season, is to have her make a store by cutting out magazine pictures of groceries. This game is practically unlimited, since a few copies of a women's magazine will afford brightly colored reproductions of practically everything to eat and drink.

No doubt, in daily dramatic play with her friends she will do a certain amount of "going to the store," but helping her set up a more elaborate play store will familiarize her better with the real situation. Besides, it is fun.

## GETTING NEW SHOES

Probably the first kind of shopping for clothes that your pre-schooler will do in her life is to get new shoes. This is the only kind of clothing that needs to fit precisely and that therefore requires her presence. It is important that you explain several things before setting forth on this expedition.

First is the question of choice. State exactly what kind of shoes you intend to get—dress-up shoes or sturdy everyday shoes, sandals or closed shoes, laced shoes or buckled shoes. If there is some aspect of choice which you will not decide in advance, mention what the choice is to be: "I'm not sure whether I'll get you leather-soled shoes or shoes with rubber soles. I'll decide when I see what they have." Do not indicate that the choice will be Judy's unless you are prepared to accept her verdict. If she is to have a choice, be sure to specify where that choice will lie.

Second is the matter of price. Related to what kind of shoes you will buy is the amount you intend to spend. Tell Judy about this, too. You might say, for example, "I'm going to try to get you a pair of shoes for about five dollars. If we see some that cost a lot more, even though they may be very nice, I'm not going to get them. Five dollars is about all we can afford for this pair."

Most ticklish matter, however, is the question of fit. It seems inevitable that the shoes which suit you and your child perfectly are a little too tight and they're all out of that model in her size. Explain in advance that the most important thing is to get shoes that fit perfectly, and that you won't take any that don't fit no matter how pretty they may be. Explain to her that she will put them on, walk about, and then say exactly how they feel. Encourage her to tell you how they really feel and not to be swayed by the salesman's enthusiasm or her delight in the style.

Unless you have a long way to walk, after leaving the store, let Judy wear her new shoes home. One of the rewards for the ordeal of buying shoes (and it sometimes takes much too long for a little child) is to walk out wearing the new shoes, carrying the old ones in a neat little package.

## GETTING NEW CLOTHES

Sooner or later your preschooler will have to go with you to buy some other kind of clothing that needs to fit—a first fitted overcoat, a boy's first suit, a very special dress for Judy.

Going to a clothing store is very exciting in prospect, and may be very enjoyable for the first ten minutes. But all too frequently this expedition ends up with a restless child and an irritated parent. Part of the problem is that the variety offered is so much greater than that which you find in the shoe store. Thus, it is harder to give Judy her choice, and harder on her if you do the choosing.

One way, if you have time, is for you to go shopping in advance and choose the garment you want. Then bring Judy in on another day in order to get the size just right. If you do this, explain in advance that you have selected the dress; tell her about it in detail and with enthusiasm. Explain, before you go, that she may see other clothes which will intrigue her, but that you have selected with great care and that this is the best one for such and such reasons.

A better way is to take home two or three sizes of the same garment. Many stores let you do this with the understanding that you will try them on at home and return the ones that do no tfit.

Best of all, of course, is to let Judy do some of the choosing. Tell her that you will select several garments, and that then she will have absolutely final say as to which one of these she wants (provided it fits her properly). If you give her this privilege, support her choice. Don't say later, "It's really too bad we didn't choose the blue one." Rather say, "There were three very nic_ dresses, Daddy, and the one that Judy chose was certainl·/ the nicest of all!" The right to make a choice, if it is not followed by

your enthusiastic support, makes for less independence than having no choice in the first place. Independence is the ability to sally forth into a new area—with confidence of handling it successfully.

You may often, in a clothing store as elsewhere, have to protect your child from the unsubtle remarks of the saleswoman or other strangers. If the clerk says, "Isn't it a pity she's so skinny. You must eat more, darling!" you ought to reply something like, "We don't think she's skinny. We think she's just right." Don't let the clerk harp on your child's being extra big or extra small for her age. Children don't want to be extra anything. They want to be "just right."

## DEPARTMENT STORES

Every once in a while it seems necessary to take a preschool child along on a purely adult shopping tour of department stores. If this happened to you during your childhood, you surely can still remember how tiring and discouraging it was. Best advice is to avoid this situation. If you cannot, then make the trip as brief as possible. Try to find something for her to do each place you stop. In the shoe department she might enjoy sitting on the salesman's little stool; in the dress department you might encourage her to strike up an imaginary conversation with a wax clothing dummy. A box of animal crackers or tiny candies like jujubes may help her through the day. A promise of ice cream at the end of the tour may help, and this is small enough compensation for accompanying you on the trip.

If you plan to include some purchases for Judy along with your own shopping, figure out carefully where they should come in the itinerary. Anything that will take patience and dealing with people should come first. This applies especially to buying an article of clothing. Other items, like a pair of rubbers, a book already decided on, a new blanket for her bed—these can be interspersed with the purchases you will be making for the household or yourself, so as to vary the trip and provide some high spots for her.

Do not leave her in the toy department or some other interesting corner of the store while you go off. Toy departments are not intended as amusement areas, and she will probably end up scolded by the clerks for handling the merchandise. In any case, your ten minutes will seem like hours to her and she will feel lost and abandoned. In a big strange place like a department store don't leave her anywhere, unless with an adult or responsible older child whom she knows well and trusts entirely.

## THE FIVE-AND-TEN

The five-and-ten-cent store, in itself a miniature department store, is quite different in its effect. Shopping here is always a delight for a small child. Holding tightly to your hand she can see any number of little things worth looking at while you do your shopping.

A pleasant part of this trip involves the dime or so that she may be given to spend. Take plenty of time for this part of the expedition; it is what makes the whole affair worthwhile. On giving her the money, explain that there will be no more. Once she has spent this coin, there will be no other forthcoming, no matter how intriguing an object she may discover later. Explain, too, that many items, perhaps most, cost more than her dime and that she will have to choose something that she can afford. Help her to understand that with a dime, for example, she can buy either one ten-cent item or two five-cent ones. She might also be encouraged to see, if she is five or six years old, that she could save the dime, add it to the one she will receive on the next trip to the five-and-ten, and then buy a twenty-cent item. If she has an allowance, some of which is kept available, rather than in a one-way bank, she might be told before leaving home that she can take along something to spend at the five-and-ten, in addition to the dime you will give her there.

With your help she can find countless intriguing or useful things from which to choose. Don't let her feel that the toy counter is the only place to look. The stationery counter, for example, is a treasure chest of tiny colored pads, pencils of all kinds, crayons, ink, erasers, and other items that she can really put to use. For a girl, the counter showing the cheapest jewelry may be important; for a little boy, the hardware department. But many objects, not so entrancing on the surface, may appeal to your child. How about a new orange juice glass with a pretty design on it? Or a wash cloth that would be all her own? Or a plant? Or a goldfish? Or something to eat?

A five-and-ten is like an oriental bazaar, filled with the wonders of the world, and scaled down to suit a child's pocketbook. It gives your child a chance to meet the world of shopping at its most satisfying, and to begin the difficult art of choosing and buying.

## SHOPPING ALONE

Going to the store alone, whether to buy something for herself or to run an errand for you, is the ultimate experience for a preschooler in this area. This is not merely a step leading to independence, but independence accomplished, and is worth planning for with care. A good first experience is vital. Care during the next few experiences may so strengthen her self-confidence as to enable her to take a set-back or two along the way.

These set-backs are hard to avoid. There are some store clerks who will skip a child's turn and wait on grownup after grownup until the child goes home in tears and without her purchase. There are even clerks who feel that to short-change a child is fair game. And there may be times when your child will forget what she was to buy, or lose her list, or drop a bottle of milk or a dozen eggs on the way home. Or she may lose her money on her way to the store, or her change on the way back.

All these possibilities you will have to guard against with great care for the first few times, at least. Eventually your child will have enough self-confidence and experience so that she will insist on being waited on when her turn comes, so that she will count her change (if possible), and will reach home with change and purchases intact.

First errands should always be one-item errands. You send your child to the nearest store for a loaf of bread, a quart of milk, a pound of string beans—not two or three of them, but just one. Make sure that specifications are well memorized or written down. If you want pasteurized milk, or homogenized milk, or a certain brand of milk, see to it that she can say the words easily and clearly, or give her a note to the grocer.

Send her to a store that she is familiar with, and if possible one where the clerks are familiar with her. It's a good idea while shopping with your child in a neighborhood store to say to the clerk, "You know my daughter, Judy, don't you? That's good, because some time she may come shopping here without me and she'll be glad to know that you'll recognize her." This will not only increase the chances of the clerk's being considerate when Judy does come shopping alone, but it will give her more confidence in approaching the situation.

If she has to get change (and if she's as old as four or five this is a good part of the experience) tell her how much it will be. Tell her the specific coins she will receive, especially if there are several possibilities: "The bread will cost fifteen cents and this quarter I'm giving you is twenty-five cents. You'll get ten cents in change. They may give you one dime, or they may give you two nickels. Either way, it comes to ten cents because one dime and two nickels are worth just the same amount."

Check with her as to how she will carry the money. If she prefers to hold it in her hand, and the distance is short, let her. She may have a tiny purse or borrow one from you. This will give her something better to grasp. If she is to take coins in her pocket, better wrap them in a handkerchief or a cleansing tissue, so they will be less likely to fall out. A dollar bill in an envelope, folded so that it fits the pocket tightly, is better than the bill by itself. It is wise not only to check the way she takes the money to the store, but remind her how she ought to bring home the change.

A five- or six-year-old can go not only to food stores of various kinds, during these years, but to the drug store or newsstand or to the dry cleaner's to pick up something small and light enough for her to carry home.

For the child who is not able to undertake adult shopping errands, during preschool years, there is another possibility for starting the ball rolling. Suggest having her go to the store to buy small items for herself. An ice cream pop or stick of chewing gum is easy to manage, for most children. The amount of money is small—it may even be the child's own—and the risk of losing it doesn't weigh so heavily. You can arrange it so there need be no change, if this is an obstacle in the child's mind. Also there is no problem about getting the right thing, because there is no one to satisfy but the child herself.

It is important, when a child returns from a solo shopping venture, that you talk it over and encourage her feelings of success. Talk about what turned out to be easy and what was hard. Give her the feeling that her help was valuable to you. If she should come back with the wrong brand or a wrong quantity, don't send her back to correct it. Say, "Oh, we've never had this brand of bread. Maybe it's better." Or if she brings something you really can't use, or insufficient change, why not simply put it aside until the next time you go to the store? What really counts, at this stage of the game, is not the convenience of having Judy get the milk while you are busy, but that she feel successful and competent in managing this part of the world beyond her dooryard.

# 8. Jimmy Travels

A child's world, during his first years, is limited to his house or apartment, his yard, perhaps his street. It is peopled largely with his own family and a very few other familiar individuals. Even if you take him with you on various trips, during infancy, he has little conscious travel experience, remembers little, if anything, about it later. So the travel experiences from two to six must be considered as "first experiences" even if he has been involved in similar traveling at an earlier age.

At least two problems must be considered. How will Jimmy take to the various modes of travel? And how will he react to what happens at his destination?

## FIRST LONG AUTO TRIP

A fairly long trip in your own car is probably the easiest beginning. It entails problems of restlessness and possible boredom, but the environment inside the car is safe and familiar. Young children do not concern themselves for very long at a time with what passes outside the car windows, unless you help them see. On the one hand, an automobile is more confining than a train, even more than a bus; there is no possibility of a little stroll for exercise or exploration. On the other hand, there is nobody else's convenience but your own to be considered, and you can allow much more squirming about than you might feel suitable to a public conveyance. You can also stop and get out more often.

To start with, make sure your child knows how long the trip will take. Allow for more traffic and detours than you really expect, and then say, "We'll get to St. Louis in time for lunch. All morning long we'll have to ride, and we won't get there until lunch time." Or, "We're going to be in the car all day and we won't get to Grandma's until it's dark. We won't be near there until the sun sets, and even then we'll have to ride on in the night."

Besides knowing the duration of the trip, he should be told other details. Tell him about how often you expect to stop for gas and rest rooms, how often and about where you will stop to eat. Tell him about interesting spots to be seen along the way so that he can look forward to them, and so they will help punctuate the trip. They also will draw his attention from a possible tedious situation inside the car to the more varied aspect on the outside. Tell him about all the landmarks that interest you, on the trip, rather than only those you think might interest him. The charming old houses and ancient trees in some village you pass through might not delight him as they do you, but they still give him something to grasp, something to indicate that one lap has been completed.

If you can possibly find the time, arrange to make some side excursions to places of interest. This will really give him something to look forward to, and something to talk about later. A family taking a 300-mile trip with Boston at about the midpoint drove into the heart of the city and stopped for a ride on the swan boat in the Public Garden. The whole expedition cost them an hour, but it was worth it as their little one played at swan boat for most of the remainder of the trip, giving himself pleasure and his parents quiet.

Some families decide beforehand to take time to explore and investigate on a long trip. If they pass an unmortared stone arch bridge, they stop the car, get out and look. If they pass what looks like a good blackberry bramble on the side of the road, they get out and inspect it, and if the berries are ripe they stop for a while to pick. If they see a side road leading off up a hill with the promise of a view at the top, they take the few minutes to drive up and see. When you yourself are exploring, not certain whether the side trip will be rewarding, make this clear to your child. Say, "Let's drive up this road and see if we come to a nice pool in the brook for wading. There may not be one, but let's just go and see." A few such expeditions can give the long dull trip the feeling of an adventure, one in which your child has a full share.

Many people expect their preschooler to sleep on a long auto trip, and probably most of them are disappointed. This is obviously a good solution to make the time go by, but don't count on it. If you do, you will tend to feel annoyed with Jimmy when he doesn't fall asleep, as though he were keeping awake on purpose. However, you can increase the chances of his falling asleep by taking along his pillow, a blanket from his bed, and a favorite toy if he generally sleeps with one.

In addition, take along other things for his entertainment: any kind of small toy, picture books to look at, stuffed animals, crayons and paper. Let him choose the items, but take a few as surprises. Take things, too, that you can do with him—story books to read aloud, song books for family singing, games for two.

Refreshments that take a long time to eat are also worthwhile additions to your gear. Get a pound of peanuts in the shell and an extra paper bag to put the cracked shells in. (An extra paper bag or some other receptacle to serve as a trash basket will be useful on any car trip with a small child. Another good idea is a bottle of water, in addition to whatever beverage you may carry in your vacuum bottle, for occasional drinks, washing sticky hands, etc.)

Whatever you take for his amusement, you must bear in mind that staying in one place for many hours is a strain on Jimmy, and you will need to play *with* him a good part of the time. Otherwise his best intentions will come to naught.

## FIRST LONG BUS TRIP

In preparing your child for a long ride on a bus, the important knowledge to impart is that one can walk about, get something to eat, and go to the toilet, only at long intervals when the bus stops. This knowledge, firmly entrenched in Jimmy's mind, can make it an adventure rather than an inconvenience. Tell him about it several times in advance and tell him again as you get on the bus. It is often easier than parents think for a child to live up to a difficult situation, when he knows that there is no choice involved.

As with a car trip, you will need to arrange things for Jimmy to do, sights to look for outside the window, books for him to look at and one for you to read aloud to him. Here, too, some kind of refreshment which comes in small pieces—nuts, dry cereal, popcorn, tiny whole wheat crackers—will be very useful.

You can play "I Spy" to help time go by and to help direct his attention to the world outside the bus, once he has grown tired of the sights and sounds inside. You play this by suggesting some object to look for outside, and the first person to see one calls, "I spy!" and is the winner of the round. He then has the right to name the next object to be watched for. It may be quite hard for Jimmy to think up a goal, or he may tend to choose one that you would be unlikely to come upon, a boy with a kitten while you are riding through sparsely settled countryside, or a cow while you are riding through suburb or city. But you can help him, when it is his turn to choose, by suggesting an object for him: "Why don't you choose a red and white gas station?" or, "Why don't we look for a trailer truck?"

It is important to remember that a child is a child, even in a public conveyance. Don't be embarrassed by his childish noises. Of course you want to protect your fellow passengers within reason, but at the same time he is a passenger too and has a right to act more-or-less like himself.

## FIRST TRAIN TRIP

A train ride is easier on your preschooler than any other public conveyance, for the same reasons that it is easier on you. You are not "tied to your seat." On the train Jimmy can walk to one end of the car for frequent drinks from the water cooler, to the other end for frequent trips to the washroom, or just back and forth for physical outlet and exploration.

When the time is long between stops and if Jimmy has for the moment exhausted the possibilities of the car in which you are riding, you might take him for a long walk from one end of the train to another. (If you are a coach passenger and a Pullman porter objects to your passing through his car, simply explain what you are doing and it will surely be all right.) If it's a long trip and

you plan on a meal in the diner or a sandwich in the club car, this will afford considerable diversion. Here, of course, you bring your child against the difficulties always involved in taking him to a restaurant, but under these circumstances the change will be so welcome as to be worth all risks.

When the train makes a stop for five minutes or more, get out and stroll down the platform with him. The few minutes of fresh air, plus the change of scene, will provide relief from whatever tensions are built up over the hours. Of course you will also need to provide occupations for the seat, since he won't spend the entire trip running about and eating, and you wouldn't want him to. It is a good idea for any kind of traveling to provide a special shopping bag—a soft kind, such as those made of string or nylon net—for the games, toys, books, refreshments, and other things brought for Jimmy's use in transit. In that way you will be able to find a diversion quickly, when necessary, and he will be reassured right from the beginning by the knowledge that there is plenty for him to do.

## FIRST PLANE TRIP

Jimmy's first air travel will not be thrilling to him as you may well think it ought to be. We are living in the last period of history in which adults still think of flying as a miracle; our children do not. Your preschooler will be no more impressed by the mystical moment when the wheels actually leave the ground, than you are by the starting of your car, or the fact that your toaster pops up the toast.

This does not mean that the trip won't be exciting for him. It will be. The take-off and the landing will be interesting, and looking out of the window for the first ten or fifteen minutes will hold his attention. But for the most part the trip will be long and dull for him, with lack of room to move about.

To you it may seem wondrous that the twelve-hour train or auto trip is reduced to two or three hours. For him the two or three hours will seem like ages. Here, as in the case of other means of travel, "Jimmy's special shopping bag" of entertainments and treats will be necessary. The only other diversions are the refreshments served by the hostess, and perhaps a trip up to see the pilots at work.

A good game to compensate for the almost total confinement of the airplane seat is "Sitting Down Hide and Seek." You play this by thinking of a place where you might be hiding in the cabin (you can assume you are any size for this one) and then ask, "Where am I?" Jimmy will have to guess until he happens upon the fact that you are in his shirt pocket. Then it will be his turn to "hide" and your turn to guess. When the game begins to lose interest, you can set another area for "hiding" and "seeking." Decide that now all the hiding places must be at home. Jimmy may "hide" under your bed and you must guess until you "find" him there or somewhere similar. Or, if he is familiar with the house at your destination, "hide" there. Besides being diverting, this will help accustom him in advance to being at Grandpa's, or wherever you are going.

## TROLLEYS, URBAN BUSES, SUBWAYS, AND "EL"

Whether you are city dwellers or taking Jimmy on a trip to the city, first rides on urban public conveyances will be interesting for your child. It is perhaps more important for city folks that first rides in these vehicles be pleasant ones, as they will have to cope with them for years to come and want to get off to a good start.

Years ago riding in these trains and buses was fun. Today, as cities continue to grow faster than public transportation can be developed, crowded riding is likely to be a struggle. Certainly it is important to choose the least crowded hour for Jimmy's first rides—if there are any uncrowded hours at all in your town. To be half suffocated and three-quarters crushed in a Washington, D.C. bus or a Pittsburgh trolley car at rush hour is scarcely a reassuring experience.

Choose, if you can, for first trips a distance that is reasonably short—five or ten minutes. Explain in advance where you will get on, where you will get off, what you will see en route. Tell him about how you pay, buying tokens if that is involved, putting the token or coin in the slot or box. In most urban transportation you don't have to pay for a preschooler, but perhaps you can have him put the money in the box for you. (Have the right change in advance, if possible. This will make it easier for you to get in and seated before the vehicle begins to move.) Explain in advance, too, the hazards that may be involved—the possibility of a long wait for the bus, the lack of a seat in the subway, the crowded condition of the trolley car.

It is generally better to have Jimmy on your lap, in these vehicles, than seated beside you. For one thing he will be better able to look out the window. More important, he may have a fear of somehow becoming separated from you in the hurly-burly, and this will keep him close and secure.

It is well worth your while to take your preschooler for rides on cable or trolley cars or on one of the few elevated train lines left standing. These modes of travel are fast becoming obsolete and he may like to remember having ridden on them when he reads about them in later life. Chicago's "El" seems destined to last for some years, but the ones in New York are on the wane. As for trolley cars, with their strange, swaying ride, and the smell of ozone and axle grease, they are rapidly being replaced everywhere by buses.

The glamor of a ride in a subway train has to be built up by you, if Jimmy is to enjoy it. At first he may hope to look out of the windows and see rocks and worms (or fish, if the tubes go under a river) and he will be disappointed. But you can help him see how clever it is to run these trains under the city, where they are not in anybody's way and where they can run much faster than surface transportation. Ride in the front of the first car and look at the track ahead. You can also make it into a kind of game, and guess what it will be like when you get upstairs to the street.

## FIRST FERRY RIDES

Ferry rides hardly come into the category of difficult first experiences that need to be prepared for. By and large they are fun and can be taken just for fun and experience. A bridge may get you there faster and cheaper than a ferry, but for Jimmy's sake it's worth the extra time and money that the ferry may involve.

Long ferry rides, such as those available on the Great Lakes, Puget Sound, Chesapeake Bay, Cape Cod Bay and other places, are the poor man's West Indies cruise. They are worth doing, not simply as a way to get somewhere but as excursions in themselves. But river ferries have their charm too, and endless variety, ranging from the hand-pulled cable ferries across the bayous west of New Orleans to the streamlined ferries found in many big cities.

If you drive on to a ferry in your car, be sure to get out and up on deck before the boat leaves the slip. Best place to stand at this point is in the stern, as the sight of land "moving away" is more impressive than the sight of the water on to which you are setting sail. Once the sight of the receding dock and the foaming water begin to lose interest, move to the bow of the boat and stay there as long as you can. If you are on foot, you can remain there until the ferry is tied up; if you have your car, stay on deck till the last possible moment.

The only frightening thing that may happen on a ferry is the sounding of its whistle. This usually happens just as the ferry is about to leave, and if you should be standing on an upper deck it will be very close and loud. If it seems at all likely that your ferry is equipped with a steam or compressed air whistle, warn Jimmy about it. Keep him close to you just before the boat leaves shore, perhaps with your arm about him.

Incidentally, sightseeing boats are of little interest to pre-schoolers unless the boat itself is big enough and sufficiently un-crowded to allow for exploration and play. Sitting on one spot on the deck and watching the sights go by gets as boring for your little child after awhile as a train or plane ride, without even the excuse that you are going somewhere.

## FIRST RIDE ON A STEAMSHIP

Not every preschooler gets the chance to travel on ocean-going steamships, but nowadays with the families of servicemen going all over the world and more young people managing to travel abroad for work or study, more little children are having this experience than ever before in the history of the world.

For adults, there is nothing more relaxing and pleasant than being a passenger on an ocean liner. Even the most eager beaver can scarcely find anything to do outside the realms of relaxation and amusement. For your preschooler the voyage can be similarly gratifying, or it can be a series of difficult encounters. Remember, the ocean trip combines nearly all the difficult, independence-demanding situations that a child will normally meet over a period of years. The ship is a floating city with countless intriguing new places, probably including a nursery. There is a "restaurant" to eat in, not once but three times a day. There are endless new people to meet and new kinds of behavior demanded.

On shipboard it may be hard to find a baby-sitter, yet equally hard for parents to spend the evening in their stateroom with all the gaiety of life on board beckoning. Perhaps after a night or two, you can leave your child *after* he falls asleep and look in on him at intervals.

However, *awareness* that all the gay new situations you face on board demand more difficult adjustments for Jimmy is probably all that is required. With this in mind you can help him explore the available parts of the ship in the beginning of the voyage. Introduce him to your steward and waiter in such a way as to make it easy for him to recognize them as friends.

Each new situation can be handled as suggested elsewhere in

this book. Spend as much time with him, during the first few days, as seems necessary. This investment of your time and affection will pay off. The sooner he feels safe and familiar on the boat, the sooner you will be able to pursue your adult desires with the knowledge that he is having a good time and that the entire voyage will be a memorable experience for him.

## FIRST RIDE IN AN ELEVATOR

It's a far cry from an ocean liner to an elevator. Parents are often so familiar with riding in an elevator that they are hardly aware that Jimmy may never have done so before, or not since reaching the age of awareness.

What is frightening about an elevator is not the fact of its going up and down (which might have worried great-grandfather on his first elevator ride). It is rather the smallness and the feeling of being enclosed which seems to bother youngsters not used to it. Of course, elevators in very tall buildings move rapidly and are likely to bother child (or grownup, too) especially when they stop quickly on the trip down.

Tell your child about the elevator in advance. Make it seem like an adventure. Describe it as a "tiny little room—when the doors are closed this little room rides up, up, up, and you don't have to climb up the stairs." If it should be a self-service elevator, ask him if he wants to press the button. Lift him up to reach it, and show him which one to press. You won't have to show him often! Many a city preschooler learns to read numbers early through operating these elevators.

Don't be chagrinned if your child finds his first elevator ride scary or uncomfortable, and don't laugh at him or call him foolish. How much better to say gravely, "Yes, it may feel funny for the first time or two, but before long you won't even give it a thought." It is often a good idea, provided Jimmy is willing, to take a few extra rides up and down at once, if the first trip didn't go too well. In this way you may end his fears for good and all. But don't push this idea unless you feel sure it's all right. If he felt forced to do it, to gain your approval, the result might be to reinforce his original anxiety.

## FIRST ESCALATOR RIDE

The child has probably not been born for whom an escalator is frightening—the problem is to get him off. His first ride on this conveyance will undoubtedly delight him, and he'll want to go up and down again interminably, just for the fun of it. For many youngsters the moving stairs are the *raison d'etre* for department stores and railroad terminals.

The only thing to keep in mind is that Jimmy can't read the signs and you must help him understand that he must hold your hand, step off at the end of the ride, not sit on the steps, climb on the railing, or in any other way abuse the device.

Often the presence of an escalator is a preschooler's reward for having to accompany Mother on a shopping trip, but don't let your child ride it alone. There are some dangers involved. And don't tell him that it's dangerous and flirt with the possibility of creating fear where none exists. Simply say, "Children aren't allowed to ride the escalator without a grownup," or, "Sitting on the steps is against the rules." Children can accept this kind of statement easily and there is no emotional overtone.

## VISITING ANOTHER TOWN

Jimmy's first visits to another town, or first visits to any town if he lives in the country, should be made short, profitable, and free from worrisome episodes.

To start with, try to give the feeling that you like (or at least don't mind) going to this town. If it seems to you that the town is always unbearably hot in summer, or impossibly cold or windy in winter, don't mention it. If traffic is bad and parking space hard to find, you might mention this as a problem, but one so trivial that the trip contains ample compensation for it. If he feels that the town is overpowering or unpleasant for you, how can he approach it with self-confidence and pleasant anticipation?

Talk about the ways in which this town differs from the places he is familiar with. This will provide conversation for the trip to town (and, in retrospect, on the way back) and will make the new adjustments easier. Mention the differences in a favorable light, not implying that this town is a better place than home but that the differences are interesting and of value.

"Johnstown is much bigger than our town, and you'll see lots more cars and trucks in the streets. Sometimes the streets are jam-packed with cars and you can stand on the sidewalk and see nearly every kind of car in the world."

"Janesville is a smaller town than ours. I think you'll like how quiet the streets are. You can walk along the sidewalks and no one bumps into you, and the storekeepers take their time when they wait on you instead of always having to hurry."

"Bedford is a mill town and there are three big factories and a freight yard. You'll see that it's very different from a country town like ours. There are traffic lights to tell the cars when to stop and when to go and three big five-and-ten-cent stores all in a row!"

"Portland is right on the river, so it's a long, narrow town. You'll see how the main street runs right along the river, and there isn't very much more to it than that."

Try not to take Jimmy to town when you have business which will occupy you for a long time with little of interest for him. Take him to town to visit someone whose home he will enjoy, or when you have brief and variegated shopping to do, or business that takes place in an exciting locale like a hardware store or a railroad station. Unless the trip is exclusively for pleasure, with Jimmy's pleasure well considered, you might end it up with something very special, like an ice cream soda. In this way you can be sure the town will have pleasant associations in his mind.

Best of all, if time allows, include some kind of excursion or visit to some aspect of the town that is interesting in itself, different from home surroundings, and perhaps essential to the particular flavor of the town.

If the town depends on factories or a lumber mill or an interesting industry, visit a plant and let Jimmy see what is made there and how it is made. Then he will have some beginning of real knowledge about the place—how its inhabitants earn their living and the position of the community in regard to the world at large. If the town is a farm market, take him to a canning plant or to the freight yard where produce is shipped or see the grain elevators (not just passing them as you drive into town). If the town is a suburb without considerable industry, you might take a walk through residential streets, explaining how people who work in the nearby city come here every evening so they can have houses of their own, lawns and gardens.

Often a town has something of great interest which is not essential to its existence but worth seeing and remembering. Here is a town with a specially attractive statue, here one with a beautiful old house, here one with an unusual office building, here one with a spring in its very center out of which a river rises. Be sure to include these spots on Jimmy's initial visits to towns.

## VISITING A BIG CITY

Children are not oppressed, as adults often are, by the noise, the rapid pace, the impure air of the big city. They scarcely seem to notice the concentration of gasoline fumes, the lack of trees and grass, the atmosphere of impatience. On the other hand, they are also likely to be unimpressed by the exciting aspects of the city, unless these are pointed out. Children tend to accept things as they are, and do not think it wonderful that they became that way. For example, it is a rare child under the age of seven or eight who reacts particularly to his first sight of skyscrapers, unless they are seen from some extremely dramatic vantage point, as approaching Houston by boat, or New York via air or boat.

The problems you face on taking Jimmy for his first big city visits are likely to stem from confusion (seeing too many new sights so close together); fear of becoming separated from you or even fear that you *and* he will become lost; the difficulty of finding time and place for relaxed, quiet play. He is likely to suffer from having to be on "company manners" hour after hour, in stores, in buses, in restaurants, visiting with apartment dwellers. Where can he shout a little and run a little?

First visits to a big city should be, if possible, very short. However, if they cannot be, see to it that Jimmy has long periods of relaxation and exercise in between short periods of visiting, shopping and sightseeing. Every city has parks. You may feel that if Jimmy is to spend the afternoon running around on a lawn in Forest Park he might just as well be playing on your lawn at home. But he has had enough taste of city life on his way to the park and will get more of it upon leaving. He needs the familiar feel of grass along with the unfamiliar pavements. Even though time spent in the park cuts down on specifically city experiences, it will leave him with a favorable reaction to the city so that he will anticipate further visits.

Remember that we mentioned a family on a long automobile trip who drove into downtown Boston for a ride on the swan boats in the Public Garden and then went right on? That preschooler saw none of the famous sights of the city, no historic buildings, no glimpse of Beacon Hill, none of the hubbub of the Hub. But he left with the feeling that Boston is a wonderful place and it will always have a warm spot in his heart.

Varied play opportunities can be found by parents who are not overly concerned with making preschool children behave like miniature adults. Watching families at places like the Lincoln Memorial in Washington, D.C., is instructive. No little child can devote more than a minute or so to such an edifice. Some can always be seen running up and down the broad staircase, finding a kind of adventure and a chance to use up energy and develop skills. Others are kept standing with their parents, hushed, limp and bored. The stone steps of monuments and public buildings are fine places to play, if they are not crowded. Let your child use them.

Don't be too concerned about Jimmy's getting dirty when he plays in a city. City dirt, with its greater component of soot, is more tenacious than the small town variety. Wash him up at the end of a play period, but not during one.

Of course there are special things in most cities with great appeal for children. Walking across a bridge or riding on an urban ferry are interesting in themselves, in addition to affording a perspective view of the city and an intimate glimpse of its river life. The observation tower atop a skyscraper has no age limits. High spots like the San Francisco cable cars, New York's Statue of Liberty, and similar unique experiences are worth while for your preschooler, but try not to include them in a day already crowded with activities.

Your preschooler may behave in a younger fashion while visiting a city than he has been doing at home. Though he may have fairly well outgrown the habit of holding your hand while walking in the street, you may find that on big city streets he will clutch your hand in a vise-like grip. Let him, and no comment on it is the best reaction on your part. Similarly, he may be shyer than usual or more boisterous; he may even resume a long outmoded mannerism, like thumb-sucking or wetting the bed. Again, don't worry about these things. They indicate merely that the total experience is rather more than he can cope with, and they are a signal to ease the pattern of the next few days. They will disappear again as soon as he gets back to a more comfortable routine.

## VISITING A FARM

Visiting a farm is somehow a much more suitable treat for an urban preschooler than visiting a city is for the country child. Your child's first visit to a farm may be one of the most impressive events of his early life. No child of two or more is unaware of the existence and purpose of farms. He knows, in an abstract sort of way, that milk comes from a cow, though he may not know what makes it come. He knows that vegetables grow out of the earth, perhaps even that bread is the ground-up seed of a plant. Now, at last, he can see some of this.

On the other hand, the first farm visit entails some difficulties, too. Jimmy may discover to his chagrin that cows are frightening—or he may be insufficiently frightened about standing close behind a horse. He may be disappointed to learn that this is not the idealized variegated farm so dear to children's literature (where a little bit of every kind of crop is grown and the livestock includes every beast domesticated by man); instead perhaps it turns out to be a ranch devoted to cattle without field crops or chickens, or perhaps it is a truck farm specializing in radishes without a moo-cow within miles.

Most of these contingencies can be adequately prepared for before you arrive at the farm:

"Mr. Black has a couple of enormous dogs and they'll come rushing out as soon as the car stops. They don't mean to frighten you, but you might feel a little scared just at first. You can just sit in the car till they calm down, or I can ask Mr. Black to tie them up."

"Don't worry if the cows seem frightening. They are the gentlest creatures in the world with big, kind eyes—but they are so big. Maybe you will like them right away, but if you don't feel like going close to them right away, that's perfectly all right."

"I know you'll want to see the sugar house where they boil down the sap to make maple syrup, but I want to tell you that it's a very, very long walk from the house. It's a nice walk, with interesting things to see on the way, but you might as well know how far it is so you don't think we've lost our way when we have to keep walking and walking."

"This isn't like the farm in 'The Animals of Farmer Jones.' They don't have any livestock that I know of. Mostly you'll see cotton growing, and perhaps a vegetable garden, and I know there is a tractor and other kinds of big machinery."

"It will be very hot out on the range, and hardly any shade

anywhere. But that's the way it is, and you won't mind it too much."

At the same time, of course, build up the positive aspects of the visit. Tell him about milk warm from the cow, or water cold from a well. Tell him something about the farmer's life—the particular farmer you are about to see. Tell him what the farmer does in the various seasons, so the present situation will be comprehensible in a year-round picture. Where do the farmer's children go to school, and how do they get there? Find out, if you can. What crops does he raise for his own consumption and which for the market? How does he get them to the market?

There are many, many advantages to your child in having this trip to the farm. If you have no friend or relative who farms, it is easy to arrange a visit to a farm whose owners you have not previously known. You can simply stop at an attractive farm as you happen to drive past, and ask if you might come back some time bringing your child. Or choose a convenient small town in an agricultural community and write to the editor of the town's weekly paper, or to the local Grange, or the 4-H Club or the F.F.A. Any community will contain several farmers who work with pride and would be delighted to show you and your child over their places. Through one of these agencies you can easily contact one.

Seeing food growing will help your child's awareness of the value of food. Many a youngster who didn't like milk has had a new approach to it after seeing a dairy farm—or even one cow being milked. Seeing lima beans grow may induce Jimmy to ask you to serve them at home some time. This is obviously a better beginning than simply having them show up on the table. Having requested them himself, he is almost sure to like them.

Perhaps most important of all, however, is the value to the town, suburban or city child in seeing a totally different way of life. He has heard about farmers all his life, seen a thousand cute pictures of farms in a hundred cute books, but now he can see the reality of it, the hard work, the rewards, the place and the process.

# 9. Sally Dresses Up

Some events are normally outside the life of your preschooler, but when they do occur they are so demanding that it pays to prepare for them well. These are the formal, dress-up occasions, adult in nature, and permitting little or no childlike behavior on the part of the preschooler who becomes involved in them.

For example, you must take Sally with you to church. There may be times when the entire Sunday school class attends part or all of a service, but then she will be with a group of children and the teacher has undoubtedly prepared the group. Under those circumstances, too, with an entire group of children present, some childlike behavior would be condoned. But what of the occasion when she is the only preschooler at the service? Weddings and even funerals sometimes demand the presence of very young children. In a secular setting there are many such occasions, like the graduation exercises of a close friend, which Sally must attend. How can you help her through these difficult times?

## GOING TO CHURCH

A preschooler may have a fairly clear idea about God and about prayer, but even at six she can have but little understanding of the specific services conducted in a specific church. To try and teach her much about the service during these years is fairly futile. If the time comes when she must attend the service, she wants to know in advance what will happen, rather than why it will happen. She needs to have some idea of the order of things, and especially how she will be expected to behave.

In starting to prepare her, the first important idea to get across is that the service is an adult service, that there will be few if any other children present, and that she will have to act pretty much like an adult. In practice this will prove most difficult, but at this point in the preparation it is flattering. Sally is pleased to learn that anyone thinks she might act just like a grownup. But— how does a grownup act?

"First of all, you can't talk. If there is something terribly important, you may whisper it to me so softly that nobody else can hear, but if you do it very often it will be disturbing to the people around us. Maybe once or twice you might whisper, if it is very important."

"During the church service, nobody leaves. Nobody gets up and goes out, not even for a drink of water or to go to the toilet. We'll see that you go to the toilet just before church. If you think you have to go, you'd better wait until the end."

Explain about details of the service that will involve her participation. Will the congregation rise during the singing of certain hymns? Will there be times to kneel? Times to shut her eyes and bow her head? Will there be a collection, and if so where will she keep her coins so as to have them in easy reach when the time comes?

This kind of knowledge will be reassuring. The simple responses demanded of her as a member of the congregation will be far easier than the business of sitting still and not squirming. They give her, in advance, a feeling of knowing what will happen. They will give her, during the service itself, something to look forward to, something to punctuate the long stillness and break it up into parts that she can handle.

It will be helpful if you can have her busy with some very active kind of play until shortly before church time. Children work best in a rhythmic sequence of physical activity and rest. It will be easier for Sally to sit still in church if she has had several hours of vigorous activity just beforehand. Similarly, she will feel better about the whole affair if, as soon as possible after the service, she is allowed to run free and play.

The special clothes in which your child will be dressed for going to church may either add to her problems or make them simpler, depending on how you handle them. Certainly it is good

to put them on at the last possible moment and get them off again as soon as possible after the service. Assume that the church service takes an hour and a half, and that for three-quarters of an hour beforehand and again afterwards the same kind of quiet "grown-up" behavior is required because of the clothes, then you will have doubled the period of constraint and cut in half Sally's chances of managing herself successfully.

An excellent plan is to get those dress-up clothes on just before actually entering the church. Many parents who drive to church in their car allow a preschooler to change in the car just before going in. All you need is the clean clothes and a damp washcloth for face and knees. (Carry the washcloth in one of those plastic bags that vegetables come in.) If you do not drive to church, it may still be possible for you to carry the dress-up clothes with you and put them on her in the rest room before entering the auditorium itself.

This procedure has another advantage, besides the obvious one of cutting down on the duration of exceptional conduct. A child who has just put on unusual clothes and sees herself in a mirror looking unlike her usual self finds it comparatively easy to behave in unusual ways. Her neat, orderly appearance reinforces her wish to act in a neat and orderly manner. If she is all dressed up half an hour or more before arriving at church, this effect will have worn off before it can be put to use.

One thing to guard against, if possible, is prolonging the affair by staying around the church after the service while every old lady in the congregation comes up to chuck your little one under the chin. Even though you may feel obligated to consider the needs of these well-intentioned folk, at this point you really must consider the needs of your child first. She has just gone through a difficult situation. Now try to release her from it at the earliest possible moment.

## GOING TO A WEDDING

Although weddings generally take place in a church, chapel or synagogue, they are easier on a child than a regular religious service. A wedding, at its simplest, contains drama. At its most elaborate it contains colorful pageantry. Here again there is not much latitude for your child's personal behavior. She may not talk, she may not squirm, nor play, nor leave. But at least there is drama.

In preparing your child for participation in the wedding, the most important thing is to give her some realization of the meaning of the ceremony. Obviously the person getting married is a close connection, someone who is important to Sally. Otherwise, of course, she would not have to go to the wedding in the first place. The momentous meaning of the wedding, as it affects her sister or cousin or aunt or friend, will help carry her through the ceremony itself. At the same time, this knowledge will make the total experience edifying, adding to her knowledge of the ways of mankind rather than having the wedding remain in her mind a strange and isolated experience.

"Today Cousin Frank is a member of the Richman family. He lives with Aunt Laura and Uncle Joe, and that's his family. And Marion lives with her father and mother and sisters, and they are her family. But when the wedding comes, Cousin Frank will leave his family, and Marion will leave her family. They will live together, and they will be a new family all by themselves. Then some time they will probably have babies and they will be a bigger family, just like ours."

It is easier than you might think for a child to catch the excitement of all this. After all, Sally lives in a world in which she depends on her parents and present family entirely. The idea that a young person should go forth, continuing to honor his parents but forming a new tie which takes precedence over the old—here is a startling and moving idea.

The religious aspects of marriage can be similarly meaningful and similarly moving to your preschooler.

Other aspects of the situation lend themselves to building up the drama. Most little girls and many little boys can get quite excited by the idea of bridal gowns. The question of the wedding gift for the young couple is interesting, too. If the couple is furnishing an apartment or house within your community, your child will want to know about that, and if they are planning to move elsewhere that is worth talking about.

In short, a little child can approach the wedding with a great deal of knowledge, not only as to what will happen during the ceremony and how she is intended to act, but also as to the deeper meanings of the event. Thus informed, she should not find it hard to take, despite the pressures on her for adult-like behavior. The whole affair is so exciting that it is worth a brief sacrifice of her right to chatter and squirm.

## GOING TO A GRADUATION

Graduation exercises, at their best, are hard for a preschooler to take. Even if big sister is graduating from high school, or a favorite uncle is completing his course at college, the ceremony is too long, too hard to understand, and too lacking in drama for Sally. If you do have to take her, you might prepare her for it, as in the case of the wedding, by building up in her mind the importance of the event.

Remind her of her feelings on her birthday, how fine it seems to have completed a year, to be a year older, bigger, wiser. Then explain how the graduation is similar but ever so much bigger, marking the end not just of a year but of a whole period in a person's life. However, to Sally the ceremony itself will seem to last forever, and you would do well to take along something that will help her pass the time.

A tiny pad of paper and pencil, or any other amusement which she can use inconspicuously in her seat will help. A package of tiny candies in your pocket may be pulled out when the breaking point in Sally's endurance seems near. If possible, find seats on the aisle and take her out during part of the ceremony. As long as you are in your seat when "your" graduate is doing her part, that is all that really matters, and for Sally that part of the proceedings will not be difficult at all.

## GOING TO A FUNERAL

Best advice about taking your preschooler to a funeral, or to the mortician's chapel prior to the funeral, is *don't do it!* There are few, if any, circumstances that can make this a good experience for a young child, or one that will increase her respect for life or her understanding of mortality. Most often when a young child is subjected to this kind of experience it is because the family or community expect it. Here is a point where parents may well take a stand. "You may think it right and proper for Sally to go to the funeral," a parent may say, "but I think it is neither proper nor right, and I wouldn't think of taking her."

If for one reason or another, though, her attendance at the funeral is inescapable, the best you can do is to tell her how *you* feel about the funeral, why you are going, and why she must go. Chances are, the atmosphere of the ceremony will be such as to dampen her spirits, and you will not have to concern yourself with her behavior. She'll act like everyone else.

It might pay, at this point, to say something of a child's first experience with death. There is not much advice one can give, as each situation differs so from the next, depending on so many complex relationships. But there are several general ideas worth mentioning.

One is that the death of a casual acquaintance or a relative with whom your child is not very familiar will probably have very little effect on your youngster, unless you insist on building it up. A teacher made a study of a class of which a member had died in the sixth week of the school year. The dead boy had been new to the school that year and apparently had made few intimate friends. Two months later in writing answers to questions about the class and its membership as it had changed throughout the year, only one child out of thirty mentioned the boy who had died. In a later questionnaire, in which the dead boy was specifically asked about, most could recall nothing more precise than "He was a nice boy." Several made downright errors, such as one who wrote, "He was sort of small," though the boy had been the tallest member of the class. The teacher finally concluded that the tragedy which had loomed so large in her mind had been an event of little consequence for her third grade. If this is true of an eight-year-old, surely it is even more true of a preschooler who doesn't endow people outside his immediate circle with much reality.

These facts do not apply at all to the death of an intimate. If a child shows no visible reaction, over days and weeks, to the death of someone close to her whom she loved dearly, we are not justified in saying, "How lucky. This death doesn't really seem to bother her very much." Rather we must be alerted by such behavior to the fact that she isn't allowing herself to express her feelings, a state of affairs which may be quite dangerous. In this case it would probably be wise to talk of the loss, and of your feelings of loss, in the hopes that she will be thus freed to express her own reaction. If you do not succeed, you should consider very seriously consulting a psychiatrically trained guidance person for help.

Sometimes it seems easier on a child not to tell her of the death of someone dear to her. We like to say, "Uncle Rob has gone on a long trip. We won't see him for a long, long time," or, "Jenny is very sick in the hospital. She's so sick that she might not get better for a long time or maybe not at all." We hope that with the passage of time the absence of Uncle Rob or Jenny will serve to weaken the emotional tie, at which time, in the distant future, the child can learn rather painlessly that the person is dead. On the face of it, this seems like a kindly way to go about it. The insurmountable disadvantage is that the child will remember and is almost certain to overhear some remark or otherwise learn the truth. Better let her know the truth in the first place when you can help her cope with it.

A final word. Many people, out of religious conviction or because they think it makes things easier for a child, will say, "Don't be sad about your father. He's happy where he is. He's with God right now." The trouble here is that a preschooler thinks of her parents as all-powerful. If a parent dies, the preschooler's reaction is, "He intended to die!—He wanted to leave me!" On the subconscious level, a child does not differentiate between death and wanton desertion. Therefore it is probably more reassuring to make it emphatically clear that her father did not want to die, struggled against it, did everything in his power to stay with her, but that outside forces were stronger and he could not help it. Whether this kind of talk can do any good, in coping with the child's subconscious feelings, is open to question. But it will not do any harm, and is certainly wiser than to tell her that her father is quite delighted to have gone off to Heaven and left her.

# 10. Tommy Learns New Kinds of Fun

According to stories in which adult authors recall their early years, children have a natural delight in exploring strange woods and fields, in picnicking and camping, in playing in the water and climbing trees. Watching preschoolers in action, however, we discover that they have to learn to enjoy these things, by the same slow process that they employ in learning less frivolous skills.

If you are unaware of this process, you are bound to be disappointed, unnecessarily, in what will look like a lack of venturesomeness in your child. A three-year-old may spend hours climbing a ladder that is left leaning against his house, but never try the apple tree that is 30 or 40 feet away. A five-year-old may spend his first day on the shore of a lake scarcely getting a finger or toe into the water. A four-year-old, whose family has rented a country place for the summer, may venture no farther from the house than the dimensions of his back yard at home. A two-year-old on his first picnic may wish himself comfortably at home in his own little chair.

New kinds of fun must be approached with some care, since any new experience demands adjustments. Prepare your child in advance for these adventures, make first attempts brief, and talk about them afterwards to help him clarify his feelings. Most important, make sure that he can come out of each new experience with a feeling of success. Better that Tommy on his first trip to a beach enjoy ten minutes of wading than be frightened by an hour of trying to swim. The wading he does for his pleasure.

The swimming lesson would have been due to the pressure of some adult.

## FIRST PICNICS

If your family likes to be outdoors and finds picnicking a good means to that end, you will do well to introduce Tommy to the idea early but gradually. First experiences can consist of something as simple as a piece of cake and a cup of milk eaten on the far end of the lawn, in a park, or in a nearby woods. Give it all the trimmings of a *bona fide* picnic, spreading a cloth on the ground and arranging the food attractively on it. Be sure to call it a picnic, so that when Daddy comes home in the evening Tommy will be able to say, "We had a picnic today!" (Cook outs come later.)

For this kind of experience, take the things to the picnic spot, serve them and eat them, and shortly thereafter return home. This will leave your child with good feelings—having done something novel and fun, having done it successfully, and wanting to do it again.

When you go on Tommy's more elaborate first picnic, involving an entire meal and more time out of doors, there are a number of things which can help you insure his enjoying the affair. For one thing, young children depend a good deal on routine, including meals served on time. Not realizing themselves that they are irked simply by hunger, they can get quite out-of-sorts while waiting for a tardy supper. Arrange your picnic so that the food will be ready for eating at about the time when Tommy generally eats, or even a little early.

First picnics are not a good time to introduce him to new foods. One new experience at a time is always more satisfactory. If your idea of a picnic centers around potato salad, salami, pickles and the like, most of which are not included in his regular diet, take along something that he is familiar with and likes, just for him. Serve this to him at once so that he can feel comfortable about the meal, instead of having to worry about whether anything familiar will show up. Once he has taken the edge off his hunger he will probably want to experiment with the other foods. This is quite another matter than being thrust into a situation where he is forced to try new dishes for want of anything else.

Don't discourage him from trying things you may feel he won't like. Parents so often say, "You won't like this. It's sour." Or, "It's too spicy for you." How much better to say, "I'm sure you'll like most of these things. I just brought along the egg salad sandwich because I know you love it so."

Another bone of contention that can easily be avoided is the insistence upon what resembles table manners. To seat a child on the ground at the edge of a picnic cloth and then insist that he act as though he were home in the dining room just doesn't make sense. If he wants to eat with his fingers instead of with a fork, let him. If he wants to lie down to eat instead of sitting up, let him. If he wants to stroll about with his food instead of staying put, let him. To some degree preschoolers have the urge to do these things at all indoor meals, and the urge is pretty well restrained. Here is the place to let him do whatever he pleases, as long as it doesn't infringe on other peoples' rights to eat as they please. This is a good release for him. It is one of the values of a picnic.

Also, there is no need to be concerned if Tommy eats little or almost nothing. As in the matter of manners, and as in the selection of food, the primary object of eating on a picnic should be pleasure. If Tommy's pleasure is to eat six bites and say, "Finished," why isn't this a reasonable situation?

## FIRST COOK OUTS

If your picnic includes cooking on an open fire, it is not a very good idea to count on Tommy as wood gatherer until he has reached the age where he can actually help make and tend the fire. He will probably be quite glad to share the gathering of wood, but may surprise you by thinking he has done quite a job when he has brought in only one or two handfuls. Don't worry about it. When the time comes for him to manage the fire, he will quickly learn how much wood is needed. In any case, let him throw on

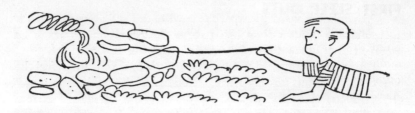

some twigs, even though it may spoil the appearance of your professional wigwam fire, or log cabin, or whatever fire structure you prefer.

There are three things which even a young preschooler can cook for himself over an open fire. They are toasted marshmallows, frankfurters, and shish-kabobs. All depend on a long metal skewer or simply a green stick, two-and-a-half or three feet long, with the end sharpened.

When Tommy is roasting meat or marshmallows for the first times, he will probably want to do it standing up, holding the hot dog or whatever over the fire. This is not easy for a child and not safe either. Show him that he can do the job best by lying flat on the ground and holding his roasting stick in such a way that it rests on the edge of the fireplace. Stay by him during his first few tries so the food doesn't get burned or lost in the fire. His first personally barbecued food should be just delicious!

Picnic shish-kabobs are more difficult. They are made by threading onto the stick first one end of a strip of bacon, then a chunk of lamb or other meat, then a section of tomato or a small onion. Then push the strip of bacon over the point again. Repeat. When it is all arranged, the bacon strips will hold the other ingredients together and provide cooking fat for them. This is probably the ultimate dish for children in campfire cookery!

# FIRST SLEEP OUTS

Sleeping outdoors, close to his parents, is far easier for a child than sleeping away from home without his parents, even in a most comfortable bed. Moreover, it is fine precamp experience. Some people sleep out with their youngsters on an occasional summer night, just for the fun of it and to introduce the child to a new kind of experience. In many families, however, sleeping out serves a definite function. More and more families, nowadays, do their long-range traveling with the aid of an auto and sleeping bags. State and national parks are so arranged that one can go from almost anywhere in the United States to almost anywhere else, spending the nights at camping facilities. More experienced campers are able to manage their nights very well wherever the notion takes them, stopping in a pleasant field or beside a brook, without depending on prepared campsites.

If you use sleeping bags it is easy to keep Tommy comfortable, but check beforehand as to how warm they are. Readymade sleeping bags range from those made of waterproof cloth filled with feathers, proof against temperatures to about freezing, all the way to those which are no more than a blanket sewed into the form of a sac. If the one Tommy will use is not warm enough in itself, put additional blankets *inside* it, and see to it that he lies with as many layers under as over him.

You can make a temporary sleeping bag by folding a blanket in half and basting the open side and one end. Sleeping bags, even though they may not be warm enough to be self-sufficient, have the great advantage of not coming apart. With the aid of a few blanket pins (special safety pins three or four inches long) you can make up a bedroll out of three ordinary blankets, but these are satisfactory only if the child gets in and stays in.

Getting in and out of a bedroll a few times will reduce it to a state of disarray, and you will have to pick it up by the foot end and shake it back into position. If Tommy is used to a pillow, take one along for sleeping out; in fact, take his own. You might also include a stuffed animal or other toy he habitually sleeps with. After he is tucked in, tell him his bedtime story, just as you would in the house. And then stay with him. Even if you are sleeping out on the lawn of your own house, you cannot expect him to lie out-side alone while you busy yourself with adult things indoors.

Of course, on a real camping trip this situation won't come about, as he will probably get to bed extra late, and you extra early, so there will not be any considerable gap in between. In any event, have *your* bedrolls or sleeping bags stretched out where they will stay for the night before Tommy is asked to go to sleep, so that he will know just where you are going to be.

Some five- and six-year-olds can sleep outdoors with another child and no adult, after having done so with you several times. A few might even enjoy sleeping out alone in the immediate vicinity of the house. But watch Tommy's request for this pretty carefully. The desire to sleep out without a grownup may be much weaker at dusk than at four in the afternoon, and by the time it gets good and dark the desire may have disappeared for good. If so, you might suggest a reason why *you* think it better to post-pone the sleep out! As with other kinds of first experiences, one unsuccessful try can do much more damage than waiting a few years until you are quite sure the child is ready.

## AT THE SWIMMING HOLE

Nothing pleases a parent more than a child who is fearless in the water—and nothing is less apt to teach a child fearlessness than the knowledge that his parents expect him to be a hero. When you first take Tommy to the swimming hole, try to persuade yourself in advance that your object is for him to have fun—whether that fun turns out to be knee-deep, waist-deep, chin-deep, or simply playing on the dry shore. Not only do many children not take to the water at once, but it is also common for a child who splashed merrily about, at one-and-a-half or two, to be pretty shy of it at the ages of three and four, only to start in again when he is five.

In telling your child about a swimming jaunt, in advance, it is better not to assume that he will plunge immediately into the water. Tell him about it as a series of alternatives. Say, "Tomorrow we're going to Warren Lake. Daddy and I will go swimming in the water, and you might like to play in the water too. Maybe you'll just want to wade in the shallow water. Or maybe you'll want to sit in it. Or you might like to have Daddy carry you out until you are all wet. But then, you might just have a good time playing on the shore."

By putting it in this way, you are not giving him the feeling that you have high expectations that he is supposed to live up to.

The old stand-by of a pail and shovel is probably the best waterside toy, and toy boats are fun if an adult is willing to stand by as a retriever. Beach balls are fine on the beach, but not in the water. Tubes, water-wings, and the like are better avoided. They don't often help a child learn to swim and they are likely to be dangerous, giving him a false sense of security. At many public . beaches where there are lifeguards on duty such devices are outlawed for this very reason.

Many parents find it almost irresistible to carry a small child into deep water. You can scarcely visit a public beach without hearing some preschooler screaming in terror while his Daddy merrily dips him into deep water. If Tommy asks to be carried out into the water, do it, of course. But try to keep alert to his wishes, as you go along. He may want to be carried out deep but held high enough to keep dry. He may want to be lowered into the water part way. He may want to be reassured that he is not over his depth.

## FIRST SWIMMING LESSONS

Children who have real trouble learning to swim at six or nine or twelve are most often those who have had frightening water experiences when younger. You can help avoid them.

Many children, however, at five or six or even younger, are ready and eager to start learning to swim. This will happen almost always in the case of those who have had long relaxed days of water play and who have therefore no fear of it. If your preschooler wants you to help him swim, the best indication of his readiness to start is his willingness to get his head under the water. It is possible to swim without doing this, naturally, but a preschooler shouldn't be helped to swim unless he does it.

The first step is to help him do the dead man's float. This is lying face down on the water, arms together in front and feet together. When he can manage this comfortably, get him to push himself forward as he lies down, so that he will glide through the water. Anybody who can do this can learn to swim. The advantage of the dead man's float is that it gives the child full confidence in the fact that the water will support his body and not let it sink.

Incidentally, you may have people tell you not to let Tommy do the dog paddle when he is learning to swim, as it will give him bad swimming habits. This makes just about as much sense as not letting a baby creep for fear of establishing bad walking habits. The dog paddle is nearly every child's first stroke. It develops naturally from the dead man's float and it develops eventually into the crawl.

Most important, in the matter of teaching your child to swim, is the knowledge that no preschooler needs to know how to swim and very few actually learn during those years. Later on, when he is eight or nine or ten, if he cannot swim, then you would probably be wise to get him into a situation where a professional can teach him. Many children resist learning certain skills from parents and learn them quite readily from teachers. Swimming is undoubtedly one of these, since some parents are likely to be pretty emotional about it.

## AT THE BEACH

If you live near the ocean or beach, where there are sandy shores and a rough surf, your first beach trips may involve other pleasures than swimming.

In themselves, sandy beaches seem devised for the pleasure of preschoolers. They are good not only in hot weather when bathing is in order, but are fine places for a day's outing any fair day in the year that is not downright cold.

Digging and building in the damp sand near the water is one of the few activities that parent and child can wholeheartedly share. Your joining in can result in bigger and fancier structures than he would build himself, but the sand is so pliable and easy to handle that your work won't discourage him from doing his share. Of course the things he will do by himself or with other children on the sand are without number. Many city children, who get pretty wound up during the week, get calmed down and straightened out by a Saturday or Sunday at the beach.

Eating at the beach is likely to be a problem. It doesn't take much sand to render a piece of food inedible, and it doesn't take a preschooler many minutes to get sand on the food. Food that can be eaten while still partially wrapped will be of some help. For example, pack sandwiches in waxed paper sandwich bags and encourage Tommy to eat his by folding down the wrapper, as he eats a banana by removing the peel as he goes along.

Another trick is to serve food in tiny portions; these will not only be easier for him to manage, but if he should drop one in the sand, there won't be much waste. Be sure to spread a cloth to put the food on, even if there is nothing to be served in dishes. One value of this is to define an area where Tommy won't walk, shedding sand as he goes, so that at least the central supply of lunch will be relatively safe.

Best way around this, however, is to eat away from the sandy beach. If there is a grassy area nearby, or a boardwalk, use it. It will save a lot of grief.

Children who go regularly to a shore where there is surf learn to swim at a later age, by and large, than those whose bathing takes place in still water. Don't worry about it. It's a rare preschooler who wants to go through breaking waves. If he plays at the edge of the water he will be doing well enough. If your child happens to be an excellent swimmer already, you might carry him out just beyond the breaking point of the waves and let him swim out there, but stay close by. It is not suggested that any preschooler, even an exceptional swimmer for his age, be encouraged to do any independent swimming in the surf.

You will do very well the first many times your child goes into the ocean to hold his hand firmly. It doesn't take much of a wave to knock a youngster over, and a premature ducking has soured many a child toward the whole idea of enjoying the surf.

# FIRST BOATING

Many children are afraid of going out in a rowboat, even with their own parents. Chances are these children have been somehow exposed to adult timidity. Many children are instructed not to stand up in a boat, not to move about, not to dangle a hand or foot over the edge, before they ever get on board. No doubt there is a place for safety instruction, but familiarity with boating and some pleasant experiences probably ought to come first.

The first step in teaching your child to enjoy boating, then, is to talk about boats as pleasure vehicles, not instruments of death.

A first row should take place with two adults in the boat, one to row, the other to hold the child. If he is small enough, hold him on your lap. Otherwise, have him sit next to you and keep your arm around him. Make the trip a short one—about five minutes or so—and he won't have a chance to get restless.

After a few times, if he really enjoys it, you can make it clear that he can sit by himself, perhaps even in the tiny seat in the bow, as long as he stays seated and stays still. You'll find that he will respond to this.

If a small enough boat is available, he can learn to row at the age of four or five. In a place where there is enough shallow water, he can row alone in the boat without going over his depth. In that case, he can be allowed to do whatever he wants in the boat—stand up, walk about, dive off, turn the boat over. The more familiarity he gains in these ways, the better he will be able to handle a boat in deep water when the occasion permits.

In many water front communities it is the custom to use life jackets on children in boats, even if they can swim. This is a reasonable idea. Get a real life vest, made of cork covered with canvas and tie it on to the child. Then you will be less apt to feel that he is risking his life.

# 11. Jane Steps Forth

The ultimate first experience in the life of your preschooler is the one which ends that period of her life—starting school. Here is the beginning of a major task in the life of a human growing up in our society. A good start, one that is pleasant, satisfying, and unfrightening, will make a difference stretching years into the future. You can do a great deal to help Jane off to a good start.

If your child is to begin with regular school, either in kindergarten or first grade, you have no choice as to when she shall begin, and usually no choice as to where she shall begin. There are, however, possibilities of starting her with organized groups where you have a choice as to when, where and whether at all she shall attend. These are nursery school, Sunday school, day camp, and even full-fledged summer camp where a child goes for weeks or the entire season.

Where you have a choice, exercise it with care. Good nursery school experience, for certain children, is invaluable and almost insures their successful beginning of regular school when the time comes. Similarly, poor nursery school experience can be damaging, not only in itself but by setting up in the child's mind a hostile feeling toward schools in general. Where there is no choice, you still have a decisive role to play. Jane needs your support during her first weeks of school almost more than at any other single period of her life. If the school system is good, use your influence through the P.-T.A. and your ballot to keep it so and improve it further. If it seems weak, use your influence to correct it.

The beginning of school does not mark the end of parental care.

# WHETHER OR NOT NURSERY SCHOOL

There are few circumstances which dictate: no nursery school. But since nursery education is usually expensive and sometimes very difficult for parents to manage in other ways, it would pay to consider the circumstances that make it especially advantageous:

When your child is an only child. Especially when a new baby is expected.

When you have other children and feelings of rivalry make life at home difficult. This is especially likely when there is a younger brother or sister over a year old. At this period, the younger one is no longer the helpless baby toward whom the older child can show responsibility and affection, but he is not yet old enough to be a companion to the elder.

When you live in a neighborhood where your child has no easy, day-by-day contact with others approximately her own age.

When you live in a place (especially a city apartment, or a shared house) where your child is unduly restricted in matters of noise, running about, what she may or may not touch, etc.

Or, to put it the other way, although nursery education may be desirable it is certainly not a necessity where there are several children in the family whose relationships are satisfying, where you have plenty of room indoors (and hopefully some outdoors) in which your child can frequently run and shout, where there are neighbors in her own age range with whom she can easily and often get together.

One other factor is worth mentioning. Your child, although other circumstances may make nursery school seem right, may herself not be ready for this kind of life. Perhaps the nursery school in your town starts with a three-year-old group; it is still possible that at three Jane is not ready. This is not surprising, if you consider that some children start to walk at eight months and others at sixteen. One has taken exactly twice as long as the other, but this is no indication that one or the other will eventually be better at walking, or at anything else. (On another level, one girl may marry at sixteen, another at thirty, with no indication which will have the more successful marriage.) Some children become ready later than others for the special demands of group living—sharing equipment, sharing the attention of adults, living up to the limitations (such as being quiet at certain fixed times), coping with a lively social environment for hours at a time.

If you recognize that Jane is not ready for nursery school, or if the director of the school reaches that decision, don't be chagrinned. In six months or a year she may be ready, and life is long.

## CHOOSING A NURSERY SCHOOL

No nursery school at all is better than a bad one. Should your town have but one, you must consider not only whether nursery education is desirable for your child, but also whether the available school will give her what she needs to get out of it. Where there are several nursery schools, you should take plenty of time in deciding which one is right.

Take your time in judging a school. Talk with the director and observe the school in action. If observation is not permitted, you might well question why not? Does the director feel that it is hard on children having strangers about (though there is some evidence to show that children in a good nursery setup are just about oblivious to visitors)—or is she not sufficiently sure of what is going on in the playrooms to risk exposing them to a visitor? This you will have to decide.

If you do get permission to observe, stay with one group for at least half an hour. This will give you the opportunity to see a number of activities, and to see many examples of the relationships among the children and between children and teacher.

The program of a good nursery school should devote more than half the time to activities in which individuals, or small groups, are free to use a variety of equipment as they choose. Thus you should most often see some children using blocks, others playing with doll equipment, others painting, with enough freedom so a child can move from one activity to another, or from one group to another.

The room should be furnished in such a way that few if any areas are prohibited to the children. In any child's home there are

bound to be more things belonging to others than to him, and countless things he may not touch. A nursery school should be set up so that just about everything in it is available to the children.

The important equipment should be what educators call "unstructured." That is, they should be things which can be used in a variety of ways, according to the needs and imagination of various children. A toy truck is always a truck, but unit blocks can be built to represent a truck or a boat, a house or a room, a horse or a tractor. A doll corner, with plenty of scaled-down furniture, can represent anyone's home. Sand play and water play can go in any direction a child wishes to take them. Paints and crayons with large sheets of blank paper (not outlines to fill in), plasticene and clay, do not dictate to the child. These, plus some kind of climbing apparatus, are the basic necessities of a good nursery school room. Suitable books and puzzles, together with whatever small "structured" toys there may happen to be, provide children with the opportunity to fill many different needs as they arise, working singly or with their friends.

In watching the nursery school teacher at work, you should see a warm person who does not smother the children with warmth, a helpful one who does not offer help before it is needed, a person full of ideas but who does not intrude her ideas into situations that children can handle independently. She should be able to control

the more boisterous children to the degree that they do not threaten or interfere with the activities of the quiet ones. She should be aware of the quiet ones to the degree that she can help them into group activities when they are ready, but allow them to be quiet and solitary as long as they are happier that way. The teacher should have self-confidence but she should not be an entertainer. On entering the nursery room, a visitor should be aware of children first, teacher second.

Harder to judge, but just as important, the children should look relaxed and at home. They should be able to approach the teacher with confidence and affection. They should use the equipment as though they were owners, not borrowers. They should treat each other as though they were friends, not enemies.

With so many qualities and quantities to look for, it is important that you should not jump to conclusions. A group in which you find every child stringing beads may not be a group that frequently is set to such group-wide activity. Perhaps the teacher has set them to it as a kind of emergency measure to calm them down after a particularly stimulating event. Or perhaps one child with a forceful personality has made this activity seem so desirable that the others have followed his lead. Again, several children who do not live up to the ideal picture painted above may be children whose personal problems keep them from being busy and at ease, despite the most expert handling. Or a teacher who lacks one of the qualifications listed above may be so strong in others that the school administration employs her knowing full well that this weakness is unimportant in the total picture of her work.

You can learn much in talking to the director of a nursery school. She can explain things you have seen in the classroom whose significance was not clear. She can also tell you about times of the day when you were not able to observe, such as lunch and rest hour if it's a nine-to-three-o'clock school. Ask her about trips the children are taken on, about how much outdoor play is provided. Try to determine the over-all purposes of the school. Do they feel it is their job to teach, or to provide an atmosphere and materials in which children will learn as they are ready? Do they handle difficult children with guidance or with punishment? How much parent participation do they invite?

Good nursery schools are easier to find than you might think from the foregoing discussion. Nursery education is new and you will find more zeal and more philosophy in its ranks than you can count on finding in your public school system. If your community has no nursery school, or none that seems satisfactory, perhaps you and your neighbors can start one as a cooperative venture. It wouldn't be the first.

## STARTING IN AT THE NURSERY SCHOOL

When you plan to prepare Jane for nursery school, make sure you yourself are convinced before you start to convince her. For one thing, you'll do a better job of it. For another, you won't risk having to decide once she is ready to begin that you would rather not send her. Actually, it is all too easy to paint a desirable picture beforehand and have her eager to begin. What child could resist the idea of a roomful of children her own size, furniture to scale, and endless equipment to work with? Don't overemphasize it, but make sure she is aware that you won't be there with her. Make sure she knows she will have to learn some new ways of behaving.

For instance, you can tell about taking her and calling for her, and even about what you might be doing while she is in school. It is a good idea to choose something pleasing to her, such as: "After I take you to school and things have started there, I'll come home and start to work on your new corduroy dress . . ."

It is an excellent idea, and one that some nursery schools insist on, to have the teacher visit you before Jane goes for her first day at school. (This does not preclude your asking her again during the school year.)

Many schools start new children in for shorter periods of time than the whole session. A morning session school may ask you to bring Jane for an hour or so a day, for the first few days. A nine-to-three school will possibly ask you to take her home before lunch for a few days, then perhaps after lunch but before rest, and finally work her up to the full day. If the school operates this way customarily, and relies on the teacher's judgment as to when to lengthen a child's stay, take her word for it. Even though you know Jane better than her brand new teacher does, the teacher knows children in general and she knows them in the particular situation of nursery school. Often parents become impatient during these days. They say, "Jane is ready for school and I'm paying to have her there. Why should I take her home after an hour when she is so eager to stay?" Trust the teacher's understanding. She is working on the basis that a slow but sure beginning is better than a fast but risky one.

If the school you select does not make a practice of starting children gradually, make yourself available to spend as much time in school with Jane during the first week as necessary. Good nursery schools ask parents to accompany the children during the first few days, and stay with the children for a certain amount of time. The amount cannot be determined in advance. One child will tell his mother after ten minutes, "Go home. I don't want you to be here." Another may make it hard for you to leave. In this case, again, take the teacher's word for when you should go.

Do not be discouraged if Jane is tearful upon leaving you. Almost all children go through this for a while. Some do it for the first few weeks and then stop. Other children leave with complete composure for months and then suddenly start crying each morning at school time. In most cases, this does not indicate trouble at school but rather that something in your relationship makes it harder for her to relinquish you. You can check with your school and see if they think it better for her to stay home for a while. If not, steel yourself and send her along. Every nursery school teacher knows that those heart-rending sobs will stop the moment you are out of sight. If they do not, the school will surely get in touch with you.

## HELPING JANE AT NURSERY SCHOOL

During the first weeks, or months, that your child is at nursery school, she will need more attention, more reassurance, more evidence of your love than ever before. If you call for her at school, don't plan to do things on the way home unless they are calculated to be interesting for her. If someone else brings her home, arrange your time schedule in such a way that you will have a half hour at least to devote exclusively to her. Parents who have a baby at home are advised to arrange the baby's schedule so that he is out of the way—or at least not requiring attention—during the first half hour or so that the older child is home.

In talking about your day at home, it is well to emphasize things which benefit the school child, and play down or omit things done mainly for your own pleasure. Most important, don't talk at length of all the cute things baby did during Jane's absence at school. In short, don't talk in a way that can give her any grounds for thinking that you like having her away at school so that you can have a good time without her, or so that you can devote all your time to the younger brother or sister, if there is one.

Don't be surprised if you get next to no information as to how the school day went. Most preschoolers can remember only one thing that happened to be outstanding, and if you take them literally you arrive at the opinion that they do nothing all day. (Of course, when your child reaches the age of nine or ten he will support that belief. Ask *him* what he did in school that day and he'll reply, "Oh, nothing.") Thus Jane might describe her day by saying, "We looked at a caterpillar in the yard," or her comment may be this enlightening: "Suzie wore red suspenders today."

Even if you give leads, you probably won't get much information. Try asking, "Did you build with blocks today?" and the answer may merely be yes or no. Say, "I hear you had a trip to the firehouse. What did you see there?" Answer: "Everything." Or the answer could be, "I patted a dog," or, "Joey found a feather," meaning on the way to or from the firehouse.

Your way of finding out what really goes on is to keep familiar with the program of the school, through the director and Jane's teacher, and by occasional visits to school. Even by visiting, however, you cannot get a good picture of how Jane reacts to the activities or how she relates to other children, because she will be reacting in special ways caused by your presence. In the long run, you will have to rely on the picture painted by her teacher.

Oftentimes Jane may complain about school in general, or have more specific complaints, such as that the teacher never helps her or that a certain child bullies her. Although you obviously have to be sympathetic, don't accept her complaints too readily as being literal truth. Many a nursery school parent (or regular school parent, for that matter) gets upset about such an accusation as, "All the kids pick on me and the teacher won't do anything about it." If you accept this as true, you simply reinforce any feelings of hostility toward the other children or the teacher that may exist in your child's mind. Some parents are so eager to support their children's complaints, that the children are left with the feeling that the school is a poor place. This makes it almost impossible for the child to progress in the situation. She is given the feeling that by cooperating she is giving in to wrongness and that by being uncooperative she is standing up for the right.

More often than not, as in the matter of her crying when leaving you in the morning, the complaining problem may lie in her feelings about you and her position in the home, rather than in any occurrence at school.

Best technique is to help Jane make her accusations highly specific:

"Which children pick on you? Tell me their names."

"Which ones picked on you *today.* Just today, not other times."

"Henry? Tell me exactly what he did, because I don't know just what you mean by 'picking on.' "

"You say Miss Jennings wouldn't help you. When you asked her to help you, what exactly did you say? What did she say?" Etc.

If from her answers you think that her feelings may be based on facts, say something like, "Well, it doesn't sound like the worst thing in the world, but why don't I stop in tomorrow before school and talk to Miss Jennings about it? I'll tell you in the afternoon what she says."

Do not go first to the director. She is a last recourse only if, after an honest attempt on your part to deal with Miss Jennings, you are convinced that a situation exists and she is unable or unwilling to handle the situation. And when you go to Miss Jennings, be sure not to bring up the question in a tone which makes her feel that you have already made up your mind and that she stands convicted. Why not start out something like this: "Jane feels that she has troubles in school. I'm sure you are aware of the situation, but she will feel better about it if she knows we have talked it over. She feels that . . ."

## ENTERING SUNDAY SCHOOL

Sunday school depends somewhat on the strength of the parents' religious convictions. Some parents want to enter their children as soon as they attain the age of the youngest group taken. Others, especially those living in a big city, where there may be several churches of the same denomination, will want their child to delay starting. For still others, even those who are affiliated with a congregation, the choice may be whether or not to send the child to Sunday school at all.

If the Sunday school starts with preschool age groups, it should live up to most of the qualifications listed above for nursery schools. This is not so urgent, of course, since it involves only a few hours a week, as compared with the fifteen to thirty hours a week of nursery school attendance, but if the result of a program not suitably devised for preschoolers is to make your child hate Sunday school, the result may be permanently harmful.

There is one factor in Sunday school which should not be overlooked. If the Sunday school in your church is not satisfactory, you can more easily effect a change than in any other school system. Offer yourself as a teacher (though preferably not of the group in which your child is enrolled) and persuade other enlightened parents to do the same, as vacancies occur. Also, you might get together with other parents in the church to form a P.-T.A. type of organization for the church school, if none exists.

One thing is sure. However important may be the religious message the Sunday school teacher wishes to get across, it will not get across to your child if her hour in school is filled with fear, restlessness, boredom or hostility. Many Sunday schools are so well run that they serve as models to the nursery schools and elementary schools of the community. You can help make yours be that kind of institution.

## ENTERING SUMMER DAY CAMP

The choice of whether or not to send a preschooler to summer day camp, and sometimes which day camp to select, lies fully with the parents. A day camp which enrolls preschoolers should have a program similar to that of a nursery school, with most of the activities geared to outdoors. Furthermore, it should have counselors whose attitude toward children and whose feelings about the role of group life for young children are similar to those held by nursery school personnel.

This may be hard to find. If you live in a city where there arc a number of day camps, look for one run by the staff of a reputable nursery school. If you live in a small town where the day camp has been established, or is being planned, as a community service endeavor, you can use your influence to see that the program for preschoolers is suited to their needs.

What you have to avoid is undue emphasis on sports, undue emphasis on competitive games (and a competitive atmosphere that can spread into arts, crafts, music, general behavior), undue emphasis on highly organized group activities. Avoid the day camp where children are expected to live up to the program and facilities, rather than to have a healthy, happy time with the aid of the program and facilities. For example, many a day camp having acquired a pony feels that it has failed unless every child rides the pony every week—even one not yet ready for pony riding.

Since a satisfactory day camp for preschoolers is actually an outdoor nursery school, all the remarks about helping your child through his initial days and weeks at nursery school apply here too.

## OFF TO SUMMER CAMP

Comparatively few summer camps, where children go and stay for several weeks or the entire season, are as yet available to preschool children. However, since there are some camps set up for preschoolers, and others which take five- or six-year-olds although they are basically set up for older children, a few words on the subject are in order.

Everything that was said about nursery schools, and all that was said about day camps, must apply to the summer camp. In this case it is even more urgent that everything be just right, because this is a twenty-four hour a day situation. The counselors must know how to help a child feel happy and secure not only in a number of activities, but at three meals a day, through bathing and toileting and going to bed.

Look for a camp which is either set up exclusively for young children, or one where the youngest children have quite separate facilities and activities.

Look for a camp run by educators with nursery school background or interests.

Look for a camp which employs a considerable percentage of counselors with nursery school or primary grade teaching experience.

Look for a camp that is co-ed, a camp for boys and girls together, not a so-called brother-sister camp where the contacts between boys and girls are few and highly structured.

Sending a preschooler away to camp is a very serious business. Use every means at your disposal to check up on the camp. Ask the director for the names of other parents, and contact them.

Check with your nursery school director, the elementary school principal, or other persons in your community who are in a position to know.

If you do send your child to camp, prepare her as you would for nursery school. Tell her a good deal about the program, the things she will do, the new skills she may develop. Make sure she knows that your idea is primarily that she should have a marvelous time rather than that she should learn to swim or make her bed. Let her know that you will miss her a great deal—and that she will miss you, too, for the first few days especially. Talk about plans for your own life while she is gone in terms of routine affairs;

don't talk about the glorious little private vacation trip Mother and Dad will have while Jane is safely away in camp.

When you write to her, emphasize the same things. Don't dwell on missing her, but mention it. Tell a little about your doings, stressing everyday events and underplaying glamorous episodes which will make her feel cheated. Write especially about her activities, commenting on those you know about, asking questions which show your lively interest, even though the questions won't really get answers.

Directors of good camps usually request a minimum of gifts and no food at all to be sent up during camp. Follow these directions. Plenty of letters, perhaps a letter or post card every day, are far more valuable than an occasional expensive present.

It is also important that you follow the camp rules about visiting. Come only on the day or days prescribed and at the correct time. If you do otherwise you are more likely to embarrass Jane than to please her.

Don't be concerned if the first letter sounds homesick. Any child has homesick moments during the first days away, but they occur mainly under a few well-defined circumstances—at rest hour, at bedtime, at "slow" moments in between activities. These feelings appear in the letters she will dictate to a counselor, without any mention of all the wonderful, un-homesick hours. Don't worry. If it should be serious, the camp director would get in touch with you, or add a note to the letters.

In general, it is best not to consider camp for your preschooler unless your summer requirements are such that a reasonably good time for Jane seems out of the question, and unless you find a camp in which you feel one hundred per cent confident.

## STARTING SCHOOL

Your child will have an easier beginning at school if your community provides a kindergarten for five-year-olds than if she starts directly in the first grade at six. It will also be easier if she has had some previous experience with groups of children her own age, whether this came about through nursery school or camp or simply because you are lucky enough to have lots of children in your neighborhood who have played together well over the years. But whether or not she has had these advantages, whether she is entering school as a kindergartner or a first grader, this beginning of school is one of the great events of her life. It is like graduating from college, like getting married, like becoming a vice president of your company.

In order to prepare your child for school, you have to know what school is like. And schools today not only differ a good deal from the ones you attended, but they differ very much from one another. Many schools have orientation meetings for mothers in the Spring prior to the Fall in which their children will enter school. Others send out mimeographed or printed material describing the program so that parents will be able to prepare children intelligently. If your school system does neither of these, you might suggest to the principal or to the P.-T.A, that they would be helpful. As for your immediate needs, arrange to visit the school the previous Spring so that you will be able to help Jane know what to expect. Be sure to visit the kindergarten or first grade room.

The best long-range preparation for starting school, however, begins at birth. Bring up your child in such a way that she generally feels competent rather than incompetent, able rather than awkward, successful rather than failing. These feelings depend on the way a child is treated and on the provision of kinds of experience in which she can be successful. (Most of this book is about those areas.) Special effort in this direction during the summer prior to Jane's entering school will mean more than any talking about school. Let it be a wonderful summer, filled with pleasant events which have been planned with her capabilities in mind. A summer in which she most often feels good about herself, feels herself to be strong and skillful, knows herself to be enjoyed as well as enjoying—this will send her off that day in September ready for a good first day, first week, first year in school.

Don't use school as a threat! So many parents find themselves saying, "You won't be able to talk back like that when you get to school!" "Don't squirm about at the table. If you squirm in school you'll really catch it." "I'd like to see what would happen if you made that much noise in your classroom when you get to school." Remarks like these not only make your child feel that school is some kind of jail, but also that she already has ingrained habits which will make her school life unsuccessful.

Give her the feeling that you know each day will be a good day. Tell her she will do many interesting things and some hard things, but none too hard for her in the long run. Tell her that each day she will learn a little something, even though she may not always be aware of it. Tell her that learning happens in different ways. Sometimes she will be able to say, "Now I know something important that I didn't know ten minutes ago," or, "Now I can do something pretty well that I couldn't do at all a week ago." But at other times her learning will be like the hour hand of a clock—you can't see it move, but it's always moving.

Let her know that she will be learning while she is having fun. Otherwise she may feel cheated when she discovers that nearly everything in kindergarten and a great deal in a good first grade seems like play. A child who has been led to expect austerity in school will have her enjoyment of this play (and her learning from it, too) diminished by feelings of guilt.

You need not worry about clothing. Five- and six-year-olds do not have the desire, so common at nine or ten, to dress like everyone else. A new set of clothes the opening day might be pleasantly symbolic, but in general children at this age do not care about style or about mends and patches.

It is a good idea to equip your child with positive knowledge of her address and phone number. If she can print her name, properly spelled, it might be helpful, but don't push for it. It isn't important.

If she is to go and come from school by herself, accompany her until she feels confident about the way, about street crossings, and so on. Do not continue to take her or call for her longer than she needs. A superfluous mama is sometimes very embarrassing to a "big" first grader. On the other hand, being called for occasionally, in order to go off for something special, after she has been coming home by herself for a while, can be very thrilling.

As in the case of nursery school, you won't learn very much about what happens at school from Jane. You will learn from conferences with the teacher, and from the time the teacher visits your home. You will learn from class parents meetings and from the regular P.-T.A. meetings. If things seem to be going wrong, encourage your child but don't react too strongly to her complaints until you have had a chance to check on them.

You can help your child with his school work by making her life outside of school interesting. Family trips on Saturdays or Sundays, and dinner table conversations in which she can be included, will be worth more than homemade reading lessons or unsolicited help in writing or basic arithmetic. If Jane needs more practice in some skill than the school can provide, her teacher will request your help. She will show you enough about her methods so that what you do won't conflict with what is being done in school.

But this hardly enters into a discussion of the beginning of school, since schools no longer expect every child to do the same things at the same moment, including starting to read during the first days of school. You can no more reasonably say to thirty six-year-olds, "You will all start to read today," than you could take thirty nine-month-old babies and say, "You will all start to walk today," or tell thirty eighteen-year-old girls, "You must all get married this year, or you fail!"

Despite the vitriolic propaganda to the contrary, schools teach reading and writing more successfully than ever before. If as many poor readers show up in high school today as fifty years ago, this is more than compensated for by the fact that today all children *go* to high school while fifty years ago the weaker half never entered those exclusive doors.

Chances are your school will do a good job. But parents must remember that their jobs are not ended when Jane starts school. If ever you went out of your way to make Jane's life agreeable, now more than ever you must do so. She will have less time at home, now, but that time should be warm and pleasant. She gives you up now, for six hours or so a day. See to it that she gets a lot of you in the hours that remain. If she needs help in arranging her afternoon play with other children, help her. Let the family evenings be pleasant for her. Make the week-ends exciting. A good first year in school means a good first year in and out of school. In terms of the number of hours available, the job is still largely yours.